rest

living sabbath every day

Shannon C. Deal

Scriptures taken from the Holy Bible, New International Version®, NIV®.
Copyright © 1973, 1978, 1984, 2011 by Biblica, Inc.™ Used by permission of
Zondervan. All rights reserved worldwide (www.zondervan.com). The
"NIV" and "New International Version" are trademarks registered in the
United States Patent and Trademark Office by Biblica, Inc.™

ISBN-10: 1494206420
ISBN-13: 978-1494206420

*To Carlton, who inspired this book
and encourages me onwards*

CONTENTS

FOREWORD AND ACKNOWLEDGEMENTS

In October 2004, while we were on a training retreat with our mission organisation, my husband Carlton was asked to do a morning devotional. He spoke on Hebrews 3:7-4:11, and asked me to come up with a dramatization of the backstory to the text, of the Hebrews in the desert of Sinai. As he explained to me what he was going to say—about resting first in God and then working out of that rest—I had one of those rare sensations of thinking a new and profound thought, one that could change my life. It has, though it played out over a long time.

Later on, after we had started The Well, a Christian community of faith and mission in Brussels, Belgium, I remembered this experience with Hebrews 4, and thought that maybe we should explore it further, together. We spent a month or so studying the text in our church, and I wrote a daily devotional based on those studies for our community (which became the starting point for this book). In the process, this concept was driven deeper into my own heart. And I also began to see that though rest was not a topic talked about by many, except in a physical sense or a superficial way, it was something for which we all hungered.

I don't have this down. I get just as anxious and self-reliant as the next person. But the times when I am consciously applying these concepts, they transform my life. I am convinced that rest begins in the mind and heart, with a right view of God and what he has done. Only then can it be worked out properly at a practical level—something I continue to explore for myself.

I am very thankful to my husband Carlton Deal for his input that started all this, and also for the concept of the Sabbath symphony in Chapter 12 that was his. I am also grateful to The Well for giving me the chance to study and share Scripture with our community. And I am appreciative of the encouragement I received from others on this project, among them Mary DeMuth, Adriana Drews, Denise Zaman, and Beth Pilkington. This is not a solo effort. I hope we can all learn together through this how to find a deeper rest.

Prologue: Stories of the Rest-Deprived

Robert grew up in a home with an alcoholic father whose addictions caused him to lose multiple jobs over the course of his life. Robert's mother constantly tried to make up for this, working various low-paying jobs to keep him and his brother fed and clothed. When he got married, Robert swore that he would never be like his father, and as a result is a strict abstainer from alcohol. He has risen in his job by being the first one there and the last to leave, and he earns a reasonable salary, with a nice house and money in a savings account for a rainy day. But he cannot understand why his wife is so unhappy, or why she so often pressures him to come home before the kids are in bed or not to bring work home on the weekend. Someday, when he knows that he has enough money to make sure that the kids can go to college with no problem, and that they have enough to ensure a good retirement, he can cut back on hours. But for now—she needs to understand that he is just trying to ensure their family's security.

ﷲ

Jane is a stay-at-home mom and proud of it. She just knows that God is more pleased with her than her next-door neighbour Maria, who claims to be a Christian but has her kids in a nursery every morning while she works. Jane holds on to the fact that she is protecting her kids not only from the germs of day care but from the evil influences of the outside world; she would never take her kids anywhere where they might encounter evil or ugliness. She reads books that says she is doing all the right things—and yet she often feels guilty about the times she gets angry and screams at her kids, and the barely-acknowledged resentment she has when she thinks of all she gave up to be at home: her job, the extra income, time to herself, subjects to talk about other than potty training and food allergies. She often feels exhausted and isolated, but then she reminds herself that God just has to be pleased with her when he sees how hard she is working, and how much better she is than so many other Christian mothers.

ﷲ

Bill hates his job. He handles sales accounts for a paper company, but he dislikes his boss, and feels like he is going nowhere. I mean, how exciting is selling paper? If the truth were told, his real interest in life is football—both following his professional team and playing in his club on the weekends. His goal at work is to make enough money to support himself, his club membership, his trips to games in other cities, his evenings at the pub with his football buddies, and a little money over to play the pools. In fact, if there is nothing really pressing at work and he can get away with it, he will download games on his computer and watch them at his desk—with his finger on the "Escape" key in case the boss comes by. I mean, a guy's got to have a little relaxation, doesn't he? He thinks of himself as a Christian, but somehow faith seems pretty tame compared with football.

Alice is an artist, and as such is occasionally... a bit absent-minded. This bothers her, as she seeks to be as responsible as she can in her job as a private children's art teacher. Her Christian parents sought to impress on her the importance of being organized and a good steward of time and resources given by God. As a result, she goes through life feeling rather guilty about the time that she seems to waste on new creative ideas rather than building her business and clients, and the fact that her finances are in shambles. There are several students from whom she has forgotten to ask payment for some time, and now she is too embarrassed to go back to the parents and admit her oversight. She seeks to make a schedule every week and stick to it, but it never seems like she is able to get around to dealing with the things she finds difficult, like money. Her guilt also interferes with her morning quiet time as, each time she has one, she feels guilty about all of the ones she has missed and spends half the time apologizing to God for having let him down. She loves teaching, she loves art, it's obviously the right job for her—so why is she so unhappy and tired?

Phoebe knows her job at a Christian aid agency is important—that's why she took it. It is a chance to help people who are really in need. But recently, a co-worker left and there have not yet been the resources to replace her. As a result, Phoebe has gradually taken on more and more of her former co-worker's responsibilities. She has the necessary skills and knowledge to do this crucial task, and is afraid that if she does not take it on, no one will be able to do the work as it needs to be done. Her boss is happy with her diligence and is talking of promoting her—as long as she keeps up the good work. But her days are getting longer and longer, and she finds herself coming back to the apartment late in the evening to do the same thing every night: a frozen pizza, a glass (or two) of wine, and sitting in front of the TV longer than she really feels good about. It is the only thing that seems to take her mind off of her many responsibilities and all that is riding on her. However, recently she has been waking up in the middle of the night with her mind racing, unable to get back to sleep. Maybe it's the effect of the alcohol.

علم

Ken has always had big goals for himself and he has always gotten satisfaction out of being one of the best, if not the best, in his studies. He has always been brilliant in English, with a deep understanding of literature, and a fluent and interesting writing style. After many years of successful teaching in a large and prestigious high school, he has been given the opportunity to become Dean of Students, with the proviso that he earns his doctorate in Education. As usual, he has outperformed all of the others in his cohort—except in one area. Ken has avoided maths for years and has managed not to take a class in it since his first year of college. Now, however, he is required to take Statistics for the purposes of research for his doctoral thesis—and he is not able to make the grade. The requirements of the program are that he make at least a 'B' in the course; but he has taken it once and was only able to come up with a 'C' because of mistakes in methodology and calculations. He is allowed to take it again, but it is dragging down his overall average, and he is afraid that he might not do any better. Everything seems to be on the line: his job, his academic record, his very identity. The resulting anxiety is causing strained relationships with both his students and his colleagues.

part one:
resting in God's
completed works

The Pulley

George Herbert, 1633

When God at first made man,
Having a glasse of blessings standing by;
Let us (said he) poure on him all we can:
Let the worlds riches, which dispersed lie,
Contract into a span.

So strength first made a way;
Then beautie flow'd, then wisdome, honour, pleasure:
When almost all was out, God made a stay,
Perceiving that alone of all his treasure
Rest in the bottome lay.

For if I should (said he)
Bestow this jewell also on my creature,
He would adore my gifts instead of me,
And rest in Nature, not the God of Nature:
So both should losers be.

Yet let him keep the rest,
But keep them with repining restlesnesse:
Let him be rich and wearie, that at least,
If goodnesse leade him not, yet wearinesse
May tosse him to my breast.

1 A Need for Rest: Self-Diagnosis

*Therefore, since **the promise of entering his rest still stands**, let us be careful that none of you be found to have fallen short of it.*
(Hebrews 4:1)

Robert the workaholic. Bill the football fanatic. Alice the artist.

These and the others described in the stories in the prologue seem quite different, but they are all suffering from the same affliction:

Lack of rest.

On the surface, it may seem to us that while this is true of Robert, who is working long hours and barely seeing his family, it could hardly be said of Bill, who is devoting a great deal of time to his leisure activities. But as we shall see, each of these people—

plus Jane the self-righteous stay-at-home mom,

Phoebe the overworked Christian aid worker,

and Ken the anxious doctoral candidate—

are all in need of this gift of rest from God.

What about you? Are you in need of rest? Look at the list below and see which of these symptoms sound like you:

- I never get enough sleep.
- I regularly work more than 10 hours a day.
- I normally work on my day off.
- I find myself wasting time with computer games, TV watching or internet surfing—because I needed "a break."
- I reward myself with food.
- I reward myself with alcohol.
- I don't really have time to exercise.
- I don't really have time to pray or exercise spiritual disciplines.
- I don't really have time to develop good friendships.
- I am just living till the next vacation.
- I work so that I can play.
- I am anxious that if I do not work hard, someone else will get the place I deserve.
- I am anxious about the state of the economy.
- I am anxious that I may lose my job.

- I am worried about funding my kids' education.
- I need to earn more money so that I can be secure.
- I need to work long hours so that I can meet the goals I have set for myself.
- I am anxious about whether I am doing things "right."
- I am worried about my weaknesses and how I measure up, in front of God or others.
- I must be seen as competent, dependable, responsible.
- Someday I will have time to do something more important.
- All of my plans assure me that someday, it will be better than this. But for now…

The verse at the beginning of this chapter reminds us that God has given to us a promise of rest. This promise may seem to us to be somewhere out there in the nebulous future of "someday": when my kids are grown up, when this debt is paid off, when I've got it all together. You may have even joked, "I'll rest when I'm dead." After all, this promise is about heaven, right?

But no. This is a promise for here and for now. This year. This week. Today. The writer to the Hebrews lets us know that if we have not *entered his rest*, that the problem is ours: *let us be careful that none of you be found to have fallen short of it.* We have somehow missed entering the rest that God promised us, and instead we have ended up on a treadmill of effort, anxiety, and self-soothing behaviours that do not create the deep rest we were intended to enjoy.

So what do you think? Have you "fallen short" of God's promise of rest? Do you relate to one or more of the characters in the case studies? Do you find that you have a craving for rest that is somehow going unmet, no matter what breaks or vacations you take?

In order to enter this rest, we need to do two things:

- We need to understand what God's own rest means, and let this understanding transform our minds.
- We need to learn how to live life restfully, acting out of our understanding of God's rest.

The promise of rest is out there. We can enter it.

Reflections:

- Which of the items on the previous list are most true of you? Are there any other symptoms of "unrest" that you see in your life?
- What would your definition of "rest" be?
- One simple thing you could do to help you begin to rest is to develop a daily rhythm of short set prayers. Consider using this Celtic prayer for rest each day, whether in the morning upon rising, or in the evening before going to bed.

> *Let my mind rest*
> *Wearied with thought and tired... I ask for rest.*
> *I pray for the comfort of peace.*
> *I pray for the comfort of rest.*
> *I pray for peace.*
> *I pray for rest.*

2 One More Weary Character

Consider him who endured such opposition from sinners, **so that you will not grow weary** *and lose heart. (Hebrews 12:3)*

Avram is in a quandary. About two years ago, he met some followers of The Way in his synagogue, where they reasoned with him and the others concerning Yeshua, crucified only a few years ago in Jerusalem. As Avram listened to their arguments from the Prophets, showing how the Scriptures had been fulfilled in his life, death, and reported resurrection, his heart burned within him. Could this be the Messiah at last? He invited them to his home to hear more, and became convinced that it was indeed true. He himself became a follower of The Way.

At first, when the backlash came and these new "Christians" (as they were called) were thrown out of the synagogue, he rejoiced along with the others to be worthy to suffer as his Master had. He had continued to meet up with the others in their homes, and when a couple of their more outspoken comrades had been imprisoned and their property seized, he had been among those who had visited them, and had taken in one of their families to support along with his own.

But that was then. And things have not gotten better—in fact, they are worse, as the conservative Jews of the city stir up their Roman rulers against this sect. Avram has already suffered by people taking their business elsewhere, finding another potter to make their bowls and jars. Now he is threatened with losing his livelihood altogether, and seeing both his own family and the family he has taken in go hungrier than they already are. Nobody in the church has been killed yet—but he knows that it has happened in other cities, outbreaks of bloodshed as people turn against the Christians.

Avram is just tired. What would it hurt to be a good Jewish boy once again? The Jews are a large and respected minority in this pagan city. And maybe they were right, anyway, and this bunch that he has joined are not pleasing God because of their non-observance of many of the Jewish ritual laws. He could keep his business and feed his family if he just keeps his head down. He has already missed some of the weekly meetings of the church, though he has not yet gone back to the synagogue and the practices that they require. Sometimes, though, it feels like doing so would be a relief, just to be out from under this pressure to provide for his family, to be rid of anxiety.

Encouragement to Endure

This is the kind of situation to which the book of Hebrews was written. We do not know which city it was addressed to, or which author it was written by, but the whole theme of the book is "don't give up." Here is a little glimpse that we are given into what these people were facing:

> But remember the former days, when, after being enlightened, you endured a great conflict of sufferings, partly by being made a public spectacle through reproaches and tribulations, and partly by becoming sharers with those who were so treated. For you showed sympathy to the prisoners and accepted joyfully the seizure of your property, knowing that you have for yourselves a better possession and a lasting one. Therefore, do not throw away your confidence, which has a great reward. **For you have need of endurance,** so that when you have done the will of God, you may receive what was promised (10:32-36).

They had not yet been martyred for their faith ("You have not yet resisted to the point of shedding your blood..." 12:4). But living under the continuous stress of this kind of persecution would have been exhausting. Wondering how they would feed their families. Fear of being imprisoned or killed. Even doubts over whether this was, after all, the right way, or whether the Jews were correct in characterizing them as lawbreakers. It is easy to imagine the temptation to seek relief from the strain by any means possible. The writer to the Hebrews recognized this exhaustion, and his whole reason for writing was "so that you will not grow weary and lose heart" (12:3).

It is not surprising that there are many exhortations to keep going in this book. You would expect nothing else in this kind of circumstance. The writer encourages them to look at examples of faithful people in the Old Testament—the famous Hall of Faith chapter in Hebrews 11—and most of all, to look at Jesus:

And let us run with perseverance the race marked out for us, fixing our eyes on Jesus, the pioneer and perfecter of faith. For the joy set before him he endured the cross, scorning its shame, and sat down at the right hand of the throne of God. Consider him who endured such opposition from sinners, **so that you will not grow weary and lose heart.** (Hebrews 12:1-3)

Holding Out the Hope of Rest

But this letter is not simply aimed at these people from dropping out of the marathon they have entered. As well as encouragements to keep going, the author includes a profound passage holding out the hope of rest. Drawing from many Old Testament sources, he demonstrates that this promise of rest that still stands is based in the character and work of God, and can only be accessed through faith. And this rest is not just the relief that will be there when they have finished the race (though it is that as well). It is also a kind of rest that can bring repose in the midst of the most stressful of circumstances.

Below is the heart of this exposition of rest, in Hebrews 4:1-11. Read this carefully, and continue to come back to it, as it will form the basis of our exploration of the concept in the rest of this book:

> Therefore, since the promise of entering his rest still stands, let us be careful that none of you be found to have fallen short of it. For we also have had the gospel preached to us, just as they did; but the message they heard was of no value to them, because those who heard did not combine it with faith. Now we who have believed enter that rest, just as God has said,
> "So I declared on oath in my anger,
> 'They shall never enter my rest.' "
> And yet his work has been finished since the creation of the world. For somewhere he has spoken about the seventh day in these words: "And on the seventh day God rested from all his work." And again in the passage above he says, "They shall never enter my rest."
> It still remains that some will enter that rest, and those who formerly had the gospel preached to them did not go in, because of their disobedience. Therefore God again set a certain day, calling it Today, when a long time later he spoke through David, as was said before:
> "Today, if you hear his voice,
> do not harden your hearts."

For if Joshua had given them rest, God would not have spoken later about another day.

There remains, then, a Sabbath-rest for the people of God; for anyone who enters God's rest also rests from his own work, just as God did from his. Let us, therefore, make every effort to enter that rest, so that no one will fall by following their example of disobedience.

This promise of a Sabbath-rest for the people of God would have been a source of great hope for someone like Avram, whose Jewish background would have given him a context to understand what Sabbath really meant. Though we would recognize that few of us are in anywhere near the same situation as the original recipients of this letter, there are elements of their state of mind that may also apply to us:

- Being unable to see anything but problems and dead ends.
- Worry about whether my needs will be met, and those of the people I am responsible for.
- Fears of the future and concerns for security.
- Wondering if God is really pleased with me.
- Trying hard to do the "right thing".
- Feeling like its all "up to me" to take care of the things that seem out of control
- Looking for an exit from the pressure, a way to find relief.

Over these next chapters, we will look at Hebrews 3 & 4, this Remarkable Rest Review, as well as the texts from which it draws and other connected texts in Scripture. We will begin to see how rest begins in the mind and heart, and plays out in our daily life, as we start to get hold of who God is, what he has done, and what he is promising to us.

Reflections:

- Even though it is a much more extreme situation than most of us are facing, are there ways in which you can empathize with Avram, and the other recipients of the letter to the Hebrews?
- Look back over the stories in the Introduction. Are there any of these people you can particularly relate to? What about them reminds you of your own situation?
- Hebrews 3:7 – 4:11 is a text with depth that is not easy to grab on the first reading. Take time to reread the whole thing slowly, or at least the section reproduced in this chapter, so you begin to get a feel for what the writer is saying before we dive in deep. Underline phrases that particularly stand out to you. (You may even want to consider memorising it...)

3 A Resting God who needs no Rest

*For somewhere he has spoken about the seventh day in these words: "And on the seventh day **God rested from all his work.**"*
(Hebrews 4:3, 4)

Delhi, India, was my first experience of the exotic. My nine-year-old self was overwhelmed by the smells of hot spicy food, the cries of the beggars and chai-wallahs, the cows wandering in the streets and monkeys swinging in the trees. This assault on the senses continued as we were shocked awake at daybreak by a raucous din of bells from the Hindu temple across the road. What is all this unearthly noise for? we asked our missionary hosts.

The priests are waking up the gods, they told us.

It reminded our family of the prophet Elijah, in I Kings 18, as he taunts the prophets of Baal who are wearing themselves out raving and screaming so that their god will answer them: *"Call out with a loud voice, for he is a god... perhaps he is asleep and needs to be awakened"* (v. 27).

These Indian and Phoenician idols, made in the exhaustible image of their human creators, can be contrasted with the tireless God of Israel, of whom Psalm 121:4 says, *"he who watches over Israel will neither slumber nor sleep."* His great strength and power is such that it can never run out, can never be depleted:

> *Do you not know?*
> *Have you not heard?*
> *The Lord is the everlasting God,*
> *the Creator of the ends of the earth.*
> ***He will not grow tired or weary,***
> *and his understanding no one can fathom.* (Isaiah 40:28)

And yet, after spending six days creating the universe, speaking it into existence all its variety, from stars to germs, from dust mites to dinosaurs—God takes a day off.

Why? Why does a God who never gets tired spend a whole day resting? Was he worn out from all that effort? Was he tired from talking? What was the reason for this day of rest?

An Example of Rest Rhythms

Some Biblical interpreters say that he did this as an example for us—his creatures who **do** need rest. They would say that in this, he is demonstrating for us a pattern that he has hardwired into his creation: six days of work, one day of rest. And if this is an inbuilt rhythm, we ignore God's example to our own peril.

There seems to be some truth to this. When the First Republic of France was established following the Revolution, the authorities sought to follow as closely as possible the principles of the Enlightenment. In doing so, they threw out the old systems of measurement with their complicated numerical relations (12 inches to a foot, 3 feet to a yard, and so on) and created the metric system, based on multiples of 10. Those of us who live in countries that use this system appreciate the ease of calculation that it brings to everything from recipes to running.

But the revolutionaries did not stop there. In their attempts to break from all that was old—especially that which was royalist or religious—they also created a decimal calendar. The basis of this calendar was the ten-day week. Gone was the old week, with its basis in Biblical myth! Now people would labour 8½ days a week, with a half-day off in the middle of the week, and a whole day at the end. Simple! Easy to remember!

Except that it didn't work. The ten-day week in fact was used for less than ten years. One of the chief problems with it was that the work-rest rhythm did not work well, even with the extra half-day in the middle. Somehow a seven-day week just **felt** right. This rhythm of rest is revealed to be bone-deep, not just a religious or even human construct.

The Rest of Completion

However, though it seems true that God has created us to function best on a seven-day cycle, the idea that God is merely setting us an example does not go quite deep enough. If we look at Genesis 2:2 (quoted in 4:4 by the writer of Hebrews), we see a more profound reason why God rested: *By the seventh day God **had finished the work he had been doing**; so on the seventh day he rested* [or *ceased*] *from all his work.*

God did not rest because he was depleted of energy after having fabricated the being of the universe and all its creatures. Nor was it simply an example set for his creatures to follow, but irrelevant to his own Being. God rested—or stopped his work of creating—because he had finished it. It was complete. There was nothing to be added to it. It was—in God's own words—very good. As the writer to the Hebrews says in v. 3: **"His works were finished from the foundation of the world."**

His rest, then, was a rest of contemplation and enjoyment of all he had made. He was done—not done in! He did not collapse in exhaustion, or move on in his power to create some other world, but made the time (literally) to simply **be** with the world he had made.

This Being of God is as important as his Doing. This rest was, in fact, part of his very nature as the Triune God, the God who is both One and Three. And he demonstrates these two sides of his nature in time as he himself rests on the seventh day.

Jan van Ruysbroeck, the 14th century Flemish mystic, understood and expressed this principle clearly. He describes it like this:

> [There is] a distinction and differentiation, according to our reason, between God and the Godhead, between action and rest. The fruitful nature of the Person, of whom is the Trinity in Unity and Unity in Trinity, ever works in a living differentiation. But the Simple Being of God, according to the nature thereof, is an Eternal Rest of God and of all created things. [from *The Twelve Begulnes*]

Another way of saying this is that God is both always active and always resting. His work is constant, and yet it is always complete. The "Simple Being" of God that Ruysbroeck talks about is rooted in his infinity and eternity, in his being able to contemplate his own work from a timeless perspective as being both complete and good. Thus God's rest is not from **depletion**, but rather from **completion**—the completeness of himself as One God, and the completeness of all he purposes to do. From this completeness flows love and joy within the Trinity, and overflows to all he has made.

Though God dwells outside time, he demonstrates these attributes of himself within the perspective of time as he creates for six days, and then rests on the seventh. His fruitful nature—the nature that is eternally at work through the three Persons of the Trinity—is shown in all the marvellous complexity that he has wrought, and the love and joy he lavishes in its design. But he does not fail to show from the beginning of the world that he is also

Eternal Rest—that his work is complete and that time can be spent in contemplation of its goodness, and thus in His goodness. In that sense, the time we live in now is **still** God's Seventh Day of Creation— the time of completion and contemplation.

Contemplating and Enjoying Creation and Creator

In doing this, Genesis 2:3 tells us, God *blessed the seventh day and made it holy.* He would involve his new creatures with him in caring for this creation, but he would also set aside the time for them to contemplate and enjoy the Creator and the work that he had done. He would encourage them to be fruitful and active, but also to know rest in the Eternal One whose work of creation was complete.

The audience of Hebrews was steeped in Sabbath. They had lived it since birth, each Sabbath eve going through the ritual of gladly welcoming this time of rest and contemplation. The writer here strikes a deep chord in his audience, who regarded this creation ordinance as a joy as well as a duty. He quotes this Genesis passage offhand, one of the earliest texts a Hebrew child would memorize: *"For somewhere he has spoken about the seventh day in these words ... "* It's like he says, "I can't be bothered to look this up right now— you know the verse I'm talking about."

But in quoting this most familiar text, he reminds them of the **reason** why this seventh day was made holy. It was not simply a "royal law" that had to be obeyed, with no humanly knowable reason for its existence. Rather, it was holy because of the completeness of God's work, and his invitation to man not only to rule over creation as busy caretakers, but to contemplate and enjoy it along with Him, as evidence of God's love and joy.

We are made not only to live in creation, to care for it and use its resources, but also to contemplate its beauty and enjoy its wonder along with God. This takes time and mental space, and a sense of wonder as we say along with God, "This is very good." And our contemplation and enjoyment of creation might just result in an enjoyment of the One who made it all. It's time for us to live in God's Seventh Day.

Reflections:

- What might it look like for God to contemplate and enjoy his creation?
- What are some things in God's creation that you enjoy thinking about, looking at, or experiencing? What are some things you think are *very good*?
- What might it look like for you to contemplate and enjoy God? Does this sound like a restful activity? Why or why not?

We will be trying throughout this book to begin to understand and define what rest is in its various facets. Here is a first attempt at a definition:

Rest Definition #1:

Rest = contemplating & enjoying the Creator and his work

4 God's Completed Work – Creation and Provision

Now we who have believed enter that rest, just as God has said, "So I declared on oath in my anger, 'They shall never enter my rest.'" And yet **his works have been finished since the creation of the world.** (Hebrews 4:3)

No matter how large or small the house or apartment I have lived in, one space has always been dedicated to creativity. In it you can find my sewing machine and quilting supplies, paper and scissors and glue for decoupage, ceramic tiles for mosaics. I love the process: cutting out the paper motifs, piecing the quilt blocks, glueing the ceramic fragments into patterns. But perhaps my primary motivation for doing these projects is the contentment that I feel at contemplating the finished result. I know that the piece is done, and now I can use and enjoy it, or give it to someone else to use and enjoy.

Of course, we cannot always enjoy the satisfaction of having finished something. Perhaps it is because our work is always ongoing and never really "done." Or because others are constantly messing up our work, necessitating continued repair and repeated attention. Or maybe it is that there is another project demanding our time immediately behind the finished one, with no break to reflect on what is completed.

But that is not what it is like for God.

The Completed Works of Creation and Provision

He knows that *his works have been finished since the creation of the world,* as Hebrews 4 tells us. Not only is his work of creation complete, but everything that he will do in this world through all time is as sure as though it had already happened to the God who is timeless, who exists in all eternity at once. This means that anything that he has promised to do for his creation and for his children is part of that completed work and is as sure as it was on the day that God rested.

Which brings us to one of the other great works of God, a work that is part and parcel of his work of creation: his provision for his creatures. He did not make this world just to abandon it, but in his creation planned for how it would be sustained, from the movements of the planets to the heartbeat of a single field mouse.

It is not too hard for us to think of God's initial work of creation as complete. We don't notice any new phyla of animals popping up overnight, or new planets added to our solar system. But provision is a day-to-day thing, and incomplete from the perspective of the time-bound beings we are. I may have a job today, but what if I am fired tomorrow? I'm happy to work in a ministry with a guaranteed salary, but how could I ever raise support? There may be enough energy resources in the world now, but what will it be like when my children are grown up? It is easy to feel like provision for our own needs is all up to us, something we must strive to ensure.

But in God's economy, creation and provision are connected. The one may flow from the other in terms of the rolling out of time, but in God's eternity, they are equally complete. And God goes to great lengths in Scripture to assure us of his continuing, dependable care and provision—as sure as if it were there already.

God's Faithful Care for His Creatures

Look at this extract from Psalm 104 below, which describes some of the ways God faithfully provides for his creatures:

> He makes springs pour water into the ravines;
> > it flows between the mountains.
> They give water to all the beasts of the field;
> > the wild donkeys quench their thirst.
> The birds of the air nest by the waters;
> > they sing among the branches.
> He waters the mountains from his upper chambers;
> > the earth is satisfied by the fruit of his work.
> He makes grass grow for the cattle,
> > and plants for man to cultivate—
> > bringing forth food from the earth:
> wine that gladdens the heart of man,
> > oil to make his face shine,
> > and bread that sustains his heart...
> **All creatures look to you**
> > **to give them their food at the proper time.**
> When you give it to them,

> they gather it up;
> **when you open your hand,**
> **they are satisfied with good things.**

There are many such passages throughout Scripture that depict God's continuing care and provision for his creation. In the great and wonderful Creation story that God recounts to Job in chapters 38-41, creation and provision are so intertwined as to be inseparable, inextricable elements of the same story. Job's cry for an answer in the face of personal suffering is in part fulfilled by this portrait of God as the Sovereign Provider, who is aware of the needs of the least of his creatures:

> *"Do you hunt the prey for the lioness*
> *and satisfy the hunger of the lions*
> *when they crouch in their dens*
> *or lie in wait in a thicket?*
> *Who provides food for the raven*
> *when its young cry out to God*
> *and wander about for lack of food?"* (Job 38:39-41)

Transforming Anxiety to Trust

So when we are told, *"Cast all your anxiety on him because he cares for you"* (I Peter 5:7), we can believe it. And when Jesus tells us to look at how God feeds the birds and clothes the flowers (Matthew 6:25-34), and not to worry about what we will eat or wear—can we not trust that God's provision for us is as good as done?

Paul reminds the Philippians: *Do not be anxious about anything, but in every situation, by prayer and petition, with thanksgiving, present your requests to God. And the peace of God, which transcends all understanding, will guard your hearts and your minds in Christ Jesus* (Philippians 4:6-7). God knows our needs, and he wants us to express them to him, knowing that he will hear and answer. As we do that, *the peace of God*—the rest that he promises—will transform our anxiety.

Paul testifies further to this kind of peace a few verses later, as he tells them: *I have learned to be content whatever the circumstances. I know what it is to be in need, and I know what it is to have plenty. I have learned the secret of being content in any and every situation, whether well fed or hungry, whether living in plenty or in want* (v.11-12). He thanks them for their gifts, which he recognizes as God's provision to him, and he assures them in turn: *My God will meet all your needs according to the riches of his glory in Christ Jesus* (v.19).

We may question the truth of God's provision for his children when we see things like famine in Africa. I recently asked an African pastor about this, and he was puzzled as to why people in the West, who were so abundantly provided for, would question God's provision! He saw clearly that every thing people in his country had, from the meagre rainfall to the clothes on their backs, came from God's hand, and told me how they thanked God for every little need received. He was only surprised that we Westerners did not spend every day in church thanking God for the abundance that we enjoy!

God's provision may not necessarily look like prosperity in the world's eyes, but it will be enough. God's provision may not come on the timetable that we desire, but it can be counted on. It may be through work he provides for us, or through the intervention of others, but ultimately it is all from him.

Hebrews 4:3 says, *Now we who have believed have entered that rest...* One way can begin to enter God's rest is by replacing our anxiety with trust in God's work of provision for us, complete in eternity, and starting to live a life of contentment and gratitude for all he gives to us.

Reflections:

- Spend some time meditating on Psalm 104, and all the ways that God cares for his completed creation.
- What kind of anxieties are you currently experiencing about any needs that you have?
- What is some way that you have seen God provide for you unexpectedly in the past?
- Read through Jesus' words in Matthew 6:25-34, slowly and carefully. What difference would if make if you really believed this message that God was able to take care of all of your needs—apart from what you are able to do?

Rest Definition #2:

Rest = confidence that essential needs will be provided

5 God's Completed Work of Redemption

*... we have been made holy through the sacrifice of the body of Jesus Christ **once for all.*** (Hebrews 10:10)

Imagine you have spent your whole summer building a beautiful gazebo in your back yard. You have landscaped the garden and cleared the perfect spot. You have bought and assembled all the lumber. You have painted it and hung it with fairy lights. You have planted it around with gorgeous flowers, and trained trailing vines to climb over it. You are looking forward to enjoying it on warm summer nights, sitting with friends in rocking chairs, sipping glasses of iced lemonade.

And then, a week after it is finished, you come out one morning to find it smashed by vandals, covered with graffiti, the plants and flowers stomped on and ripped up.

As we observe from our time-bound perspective, the events surrounding Adam and Eve's rebellion and the subsequent consequences for the planet seem like this kind of wanton vandalism, magnified to a cosmic scale. No sooner has God finished his work and enjoyed his rest in contemplating it than an enemy is in the garden corrupting his "very good" work—and bringing isolation and death to mankind.

The Finished Work of Redemption

But for God, one act in a moment of time redeemed this situation for all time. When Jesus cried out on the cross, "It is finished!" he was declaring that humankind for all time—*once for all*—whether living before or after him, had the possibility of reconciliation with their Creator. This was nothing that people could accomplish; it was the work of God—a completed work:

> *Later, **knowing that all was now completed**, and so that the Scripture would be fulfilled, Jesus said, "I am thirsty." ... When he had received the drink, Jesus said, **"It is finished."** With that, he bowed his head and gave up his spirit.* (John 19:28, 30)

Christ's words on the cross, "It is finished" (in Greek *tetelestai*), were a phrase commonly written across a debt at the time: *Paid in full.* The work was complete; there was and is nothing that could be added to it.

It is interesting to note that John 19:31, immediately following Jesus' declaration of completion, says, *"Now it was the day of Preparation, and the next day was to be a special Sabbath."* We tend not to think about the significance of this, except as it relates to the hurried burial of Jesus, and its delay of visitors to the tomb until Sunday. But why does God choose to do this titanic work of redemption on the eve of the Sabbath? This, I believe, is not a coincidence.

Though it appears that all is lost, that the Messiah himself has been executed, that the forces of evil have won the day, the seventh day—the day of rest—is observed. Jesus lies in the grave. The disciples huddle in hiding.

And God just rests. As he did after creation.

The New Creation Sabbath of Jesus

For in the work of redemption, not only is mankind reconciled to the Creator, but creation itself is re-created. The corruption of the cosmos is reversed. And the first glimpse of that re-creation would be seen on the day after the Sabbath, when God raised Christ from the dead, in a reversal of the curse of the fall, a victory over death itself.

More than that, it is at this time that God reveals that Jesus has **always** been the One who both created and provided for the world, as well as being the Author of redemption:

> In the past God spoke to our ancestors through the prophets at many times and in various ways, but **in these last days he has spoken to us by his Son,** whom he appointed heir of all things, and **through whom also he made the universe.** The Son is the radiance of God's glory and the exact representation of his being, **sustaining all things by his powerful word.** After he had provided purification for sins, he sat down at the right hand of the Majesty in heaven. (Hebrews 1:1-3)

There is debate among theologians about what Jesus was doing during this Sabbath. Some think that, as the Apostle's Creed says, "he descended into hell"; others, that he was "asleep" and awaiting his own resurrection. A third view, one that might be supported from the text above, is that he went to heaven—the Father's presence—

to "*sit down at the right hand of the Majesty.*" (It may also be inferred from his statement in Luke 23:43 to the thief on the cross: "*Today you will be with me in Paradise*").

If this is an accurate interpretation, then this "*special Sabbath*" gains in importance as a parallel with the one observed after the great work of Creation—now revealed in this text also to have taken place through the agency of Christ. One sits down when one's work is done. This Sabbath, like the first one, was a statement of completion and contemplation, of what it was that Christ had accomplished in his death. God's eternal work was done—in the salvation of mankind for all time, and the redemption of all God had made.

Hebrews 10:11-12 offers us another picture of this completed work and Jesus' rest in it:

> *Day after day every priest stands and performs his religious duties; again and again he offers the same sacrifices, which can never take away sins. But when this priest had offered for all time one sacrifice for sins, **he sat down at the right hand of God...***

"*Sitting down*" is a picture not only of rest, but also of Christ's reign over the creation he had redeemed. He has completed his work and he is in control. No longer would there have to be sacrifices for sin day after day, like a continuous pile of unwashed dishes waiting to be cleaned. In one act, Jesus paid it all, and *sat down* to rest in his work.

And then, on the next day, as prophesied in Malachi 4:2, "*the sun of righteousness [rose] with healing in its rays.*" On the first day of the week, the day God created light itself, the Light rose over humanity—instituting a new Day, the Eighth Day of Creation, in which all things are made new. In this Light, as Malachi tells us, we can *go out and frolic like well-fed calves!* We can rejoice and rest in Jesus' work of redemptive healing accomplished through his victory over death.

Resting in Redemption and Reconciliation

Jesus said, "*It is finished.*" Paul tells us in Romans 5:6, "*You see, at just the right time, **when we were still powerless**, Christ died for the ungodly.*" We cannot add to Christ's infinite sacrifice through any sacrifice or penance of our own. We cannot add one good thing we have done to Christ's perfect record on our behalf.

There is only one thing left to do for the person who would accept this payment for their debt of rebellion against God: believe that it is paid. We must simply trust in Jesus' work as full and complete—as complete as that of creation. As the familiar verse from Ephesians says, "For it is by grace you have been saved, through faith—and **this is not from yourselves, it is the gift of God**—not by works, so that no one can boast" (2:8-9).

And this belief is the basis for our rest. For if this work is complete, what work do we need to do to make it more than perfect? This is why the writer to the Hebrews encourages us: "*Let us then approach God's throne of grace with confidence, so that we may receive mercy and find grace to help us in our time of need.*" (Hebrews 4:16)

Reflections:

- What parallels do you see between the first Sabbath after creation and the Sabbath following Jesus' death on the cross? What insight does this give into Jesus' work of redemption on the cross?
- What difference does it make when you really think about the fact that this redemptive work is done—that you cannot add anything to it? (You can think of this in terms of its contrast to other religions that require you to work towards salvation if it helps.) What is the mental or psychological effect of knowing this for certain? What impact does it have on your actions?
- Jesus' work on the cross has also guaranteed that for eternity to come, we will experience rest in the presence of God. What effect, if any, does knowing this have on the way you look at your life?

Rest Definition #3:
Rest = knowing you are reconciled with God

6 God's Completed Work of Restoration

*For by one sacrifice he has made perfect forever those **who are being made holy**.* (Hebrews 10:14)

Suppose your elderly and wealthy uncle called you in and told you that he was making you the sole beneficiary of his will—all his money, real estate, stocks and bonds, businesses and everything else that he owned. Even if you were not anxious for your uncle to kick the bucket, it would be normal for you to begin thinking about these things in some measure as though they were already yours: checking the stock prices, visiting the properties, learning something about the businesses. For they are your inheritance, and therefore they **will** be yours someday.

Of course, things could go wrong with this inheritance—the businesses could fail, the stocks could fall, your uncle could change his will. God's promises of an inheritance in his finished work, on the other hand, are rock-solid. And yet we are prone to act as though they are more a hopeless wish than being bequeathed millions by a rich uncle.

Future Perfect

One of these trustworthy promises is that God is making us perfect. The theological term for this is *sanctification*—the process of becoming more like Jesus. Paul was able to assure the Philippians that he was "*confident of this, that he who began a good work in you **will carry it on to completion** until the day of Christ Jesus*" (1:6).

Paul also affirms this truth to the Corinthians: *Now it is God who makes both us and you stand firm in Christ. He anointed us, set his seal of ownership on us, and put his Spirit in our hearts as a deposit, **guaranteeing** what is to come* (2 Corinthians 1:21-22).

Just as the work of provision is, in time, the on-going outgrowth of the work of creation, so the work of sanctification is the on-going outgrowth of God's work of redemption. In time, we will not see all the end results, but in eternity, they are sure and complete.

Hebrews 10:14, the verse at the beginning of this chapter, demonstrates this connection: *he has made perfect forever those who* are being made holy. In Jesus' work of redemption, we are immediately justified before God, **made perfect forever**; but over time, we are also undergoing sanctification, **being made holy**. In some ways it is almost artificial to separate the two, as they are intertwined in the same work of God, but this is how we experience them in time—as act and process.

God Makes Us Holy, Not Our Effort

The important thing as far as rest is concerned is to note that becoming holy is not all up to us. Rather, it is as much a work of God as our initial salvation was.

Sometimes it is hard to think that God is working in us, especially when we trip up on the same sins over and over, or when we try hard to do better and seem unable. We cannot imagine that a holy God could possibly be pleased with someone who was so much of a mess. We think that while God may have given us salvation as a free gift, now it is up to us to prove ourselves worthy of that gift.

But the truth is that God sees his adopted children not as they are, but as they will be—perfect like his Son. He has already guaranteed that that the brokenness caused by sin, as well as sin itself, will be eradicated, and that we will be made new. He has even made it possible for each of us to be his holy temple (I Corinthians 6:19), as the Holy Spirit himself lives within our bodies. How much more proof do we need that he is certain of the completion of his good work?

We can rest in this assurance that we are being made holy, right now. This means that repentance from sin, rather than being an anxious act of grovelling and promising to do better, can be a confident turn from evil, and a re-alignment with what we know God is making us to be as we fix our eyes on Jesus. Instead of relying on our own efforts, we seek instead to *keep in step with the Spirit* (Galatians 5:25). We can trust that God will complete his work in us, while already seeing us as *perfect forever*.

Because of this, we can be emboldened to follow this exhortation of the writer of Hebrews: *"Let us draw near to God with a sincere heart and with the full assurance that faith brings, having our hearts sprinkled to cleanse us from a guilty conscience and having our bodies washed with pure water"* (10:22).

The Certain Renewal of All Things

A second implication of this inheritance of redemption is *"the renewal of all things"*, something Jesus prophesies in no uncertain terms in Matthew 19:28. Not only is he restoring us, but he is also restoring all of creation so that one day there will be *"a new heaven and a new earth"* (Isaiah 65:17).

But we might think, Isn't this simply another name for a spiritual, disembodied heaven—"pie in the sky by and by"? Isn't this world just going to burn, a rotten place getting worse by the minute, going to hell in a handbasket? Isn't a ghostly heaven good enough? What difference does God's renewal of creation make to us today?

Though we may not see it clearly, God's work of restoration is on-going even now: *He who was seated on the throne said, "I am making everything new!" Then he said, "Write this down, for these words are trustworthy and true."* (Revelation 21:5) Notice the tense of this verb: *I **am making** everything new.* It has already started, and will be perfected on the day when Jesus returns. Also notice that these words are **trustworthy and true**—this act is as complete in eternity as our redemption is now.

Even though we see much of corruption and death and destruction in our world, God sends his own agents—often his people—to counter these forces. As Romans 8:19 says, *"For the creation waits in eager expectation for the children of God to be revealed."* While the restoration is God's work, he chooses to involve people to participate in it. We can choose to offer ourselves to him eagerly as instruments of re-creation. And the fact that we are already *made perfect*, while being made newer every day by the Spirit, makes us the showcase in miniature for what God is doing in macro.

This is the inheritance that we can count on! Right after the Spirit tells John that he was *making all things new* and that the things that he had revealed were *trustworthy and true*, this follows:

> *He said to me:* "**It is done.** *I am the Alpha and the Omega, the Beginning and the End. To the thirsty I will give water without cost from the spring of the water of life.* **Those who are victorious will inherit all this,** *and I will be their God and they will be my children."* (Revelation 21:6-7)

Reflections:

- What is the thing that you do or have done that embarrasses you the most in front of God?
- Just as we can believe that God's creation is complete, but doubt his ability or will to provide for us, so it is easy for us to fall into the trap of thinking that even though Jesus has completed the work of saving us, we are now responsible to make ourselves better. What kind of performance pressure does this put on our lives? How does it contribute to a lack of rest in your life?
- What difference does it make to you to know that God accepts you as you are—even as he gives you the power to begin to change? How does this impact you emotionally? How might it impact your choices and actions?
- How does knowing God is *"making everything new"* relate to our anxiety about climate change, pollution and other environmental concerns? What about war, terrorism and suffering, famine and natural disaster? What other things in the world would you like to be able to see *made new* by God?

Rest Definition #4:
Rest = assurance that God is renewing everything (even me)

part two:
resting by faith from
self-reliance

7 The Connection between Faith and Rest

*For we also have had the gospel preached to us, just as they did; but the message they heard was of no value to them, because **those who heard did not combine it with faith.** Now we who have believed enter that rest...* (Hebrews 4:2, 3a)

In the last few chapters we have been thinking about what it means that God's work is complete, and has been since the creation of the world. We have looked at his completed work in four arenas:

- **Creation** of our universe
- **Provision** for the needs of his creatures (including us)
- **Redemption** of humans and the cosmos from the penalty and power of sin
- **Restoration** of his children and his creation to perfection

But if we look at the verse above, it becomes clear to us that we can know that all this is true—that God's work is complete in every way—and still gain no benefit from the knowledge because we do not combine it with faith.

Cultivating Faith in God's Completed Works

Real faith is not simply knowing a fact to be true, but acting on it because it is true. And it is only as we trust in God's completed work in **all** these arenas that we will be able to truly rest, free of anxiety or the compulsion to perform. It is only as we cultivate this faith that we will stop mistaking the counterfeits of rest—laziness, distraction, or exhaustion—for the real thing.

How does this work? What might it look like? Let's revisit some of our people from the prologue, and see what their beliefs seem to be, and how that manifests itself in their actions. We will also see how faith might make a difference in their rest.

Robert, the workaholic son of an alcoholic, does not work hard because he likes it, contrary to whatever his wife believes. He works hard because he is driven by a deep anxiety rooted in the deprivations of his own childhood, and fear of the same kind of experience for his own children. Security is his watchword, and he thinks it is all up to him to provide it. He cannot even take the time to enjoy his family, because he is so preoccupied with providing for them. In addition, he also suffers a deep fear of becoming like his father, and is determined to keep himself in rigid control in order to attain this.

What if Robert truly believed in God as Author of creation and redemption, in his sure provision and his certain restoration?

- What could it be like if Robert were able to trust in the provision of a loving Father? What if he could see that his family's security is not a matter of money in the bank, but of God's care and protection?
- What if he could believe that God had created him as a unique masterpiece, to be moulded by the Spirit to Jesus' image—and not that of his father? (Or that of his mother either, who probably bequeathed to him her own anxiety about providing for her family.)
- What if he could be thankful for what he has, and even reframe his background to be grateful for how God provided for him as a child in spite of his father?

Now what about Jane, the self-righteous stay-at-home mom? Her sense of "Christian duty" has kept her at home with her kids, but there is not a lot of joy in it. Rather, it all feels like a lot of hard and tiring work, as she tries to prove to herself and God that she is a good mother and therefore a good Christian. This disrupts her relationships with others as well, as her internal reactions to them are characterized by ranking her goodness compared with theirs, rather than genuine friendship.

What if Jane deeply trusted in God as Author of creation and redemption, in his sure provision and his certain restoration?

- What could change for Jane if she were to realize that she does not have to prove anything to God? That he does not accept her based on her adherence to rules, but on being holy—perfect—in Jesus?
- How would it influence her sense of peace to know that God cares for her kids and wants to provide for their well-being far more than she does, that she can trust him with them—even in "dangerous" circumstances?
- What if she were to begin to realize that God provides other people, other moms, for comradeship, and not competition?

And Phoebe, who must be seen by her boss and co-workers as ultra-responsible and hard-working on the job, exhibits the flip side of herself at home. The strain of trying to do more than she is capable of doing well—and appearing to like it—causes her panic that only seems to be soothed by a retreat into creature comforts. The job she loves is losing its joy, as she takes on herself the success of her agency, and laps up praise as Superwoman. Even her self-soothing behaviours are shown to be empty as they fail to touch the underlying anxiety.

What if Phoebe rested in reliance on God as Author of creation and redemption, in his sure provision and his certain restoration?

- What if Phoebe were to realize that God was interested in her charity's work of renewal in the world in a far deeper way than she could ever be?
- What if she trusted that others' image of her could not compare with the opinion of a God who already saw her as perfect in Christ—that it could stand an admission to her boss that she needs help and can't continue alone?
- What if she had faith that God was able to provide the human and monetary resources to take on the extra tasks?
- What if she believed God was as concerned with providing **her** with real rest as he is with providing the needs of the people she helps through her agency?

Turning Knowledge into Faith to Kill Self-Reliance

For each of these people, there is a sense of self-reliance leading to anxiety. And the same is true for me. It does not matter if I am relying on myself to create my own rest, to provide my own needs, to work my own salvation or holiness, or to build my own reputation. In each case, the end result is a sense of anxiety and emptiness as I drain my own hoarded resources—and become exhausted. I may **know** all the right things, but unless this knowledge is turned into faith, there will be no rest.

On the other hand, faith in God's finished work takes the reins out of our hands and allows us to trust him with all the things we ourselves have been trying to create, provide, redeem or perfect.

For many Christians, it is not hard to believe (at least on a surface level) in God's completed work in creation and redemption. However, as creation is worked out over time in provision, and redemption is worked out in renewal, we can lose faith that these will come to pass. We attempt to take control back into our own hands, failing to see that these works of God are as sure as the others.

But here are some ways that uncertainty can be overcome:

- Belief that God has created me as the person that he wanted me to be, with a unique set of gifts and abilities, can liberate me to do what he has called me to. I can fulfil my own role as part of the intricate network of created beings, knowing others will add to and complement my contributions, instead of being anxious about what I am not.

- Belief that God is truly providing for all my needs can free me from the compulsion to build a larger and larger safety net for myself in order to be free of anxiety. I can work with thankfulness for what I am able to earn, and know that God and his people are there if crisis comes.

- Belief that God sees me as he is making me to be, rather than as I am, can help me to be more up front with God about my failures and shortcomings and more accepting of his forgiveness. I can relax with God and enjoy his presence in my life—knowing that he likes me. And it might help me extend that same forgiveness to others, instead of hanging on to debts of bitterness, or comparing myself with them.

- Belief that God is restoring his creation allows me to make whatever contributions I can to this renewal, pointing to what he is doing—without taking on personal responsibility to save the world.

Reflections:

We often think that rest begins with doing nothing, or at least with getting enough sleep. But rest begins in the mind, with what we believe about God and our role in the world. So we can add:

Rest Definition #5:
Rest ≠ doing nothing

Rest Definition #6:
Rest = trusting in God's completed work

- What are some connections you are beginning to see between this faith and some of the symptoms described in the first chapter?
- Choose one of the other stories in the first chapter to analyse in detail from this perspective. How could they *enter God's rest* by *believing*?
- How might trusting in God's completed work impact **your own** anxieties and exhaustion? Think about:
    - How God has uniquely created you
    - How God has provided for you in the past and promises to provide for you in the future
    - How Jesus has given you his righteousness and reconciled you to the Father
    - How you are being conformed by the Spirit to be more like Jesus, and will one day be totally made new in resurrection
    - How this universe is guaranteed to be remade as the New Creation of Jesus

8 Worship, and a Warning

*So, as the Holy Spirit says: "**Today, if you hear his voice, do not harden your hearts** as you did in the rebellion…"* (Hebrews 3:7-8)

A little confession: my husband and I are suckers for time-travel movies. All that jumping around in from past to future and back again, creating temporal anomalies and paradoxes… we love it. But I will admit that they can sometimes be a bit difficult for the viewer to process. Why are there two of that guy now? What year are they in again? What's going on here, anyway?

When modern readers read the text from Hebrews 3:7– 4:11, it can seem a bit like a time-travel movie to someone who is not familiar with the parallel processing of passages that would have been habitual to the book's Jewish audience. The historical and Biblical references fly fast and furious! The author of Hebrews is well-versed in Scriptural knowledge and rabbinic argument, and quotes or draws on texts from Genesis, Exodus, Deuteronomy, Joshua, and Psalms— texts that would have been completely familiar to his readers.

The Living and Active Word

The writer uses these texts to preach a sermon that will break the self-reliance of his readers, and he explains to them seriously that looking into these Scriptures in this way is the antidote to being hard-hearted (Hebrews 4:12-13):

> For the word of God is alive and active. Sharper than any double-edged sword, it penetrates even to dividing soul and spirit, joints and marrow; **it judges the thoughts and attitudes of the heart.** Nothing in all creation is hidden from God's sight. Everything is uncovered and laid bare before the eyes of him to whom we must give account.

Taking these words to heart, you may want to look carefully at the Hebrews passage to get it clearly in your mind. Over the next few chapters, we will trace the references backwards until we get the full telescopic picture. In this way, maybe we will *"hear his voice"* more clearly.

The primary reference in this text is to Psalm 95, of which the writer quotes five verses (7-11). This Psalm, which the author of Hebrews ascribes to David as inspired by the Holy Spirit, was written to the Israelites as an invitation to the worship of their great God, and a warning from their history of what happens when God is not acknowledged. His quote is below (Heb. 3:7-11):

> So, as the Holy Spirit says:
> "Today, if you hear his voice,
>   do not harden your hearts
>   as you did in the rebellion,
>   during the time of testing in the wilderness,
> where your ancestors tested and tried me,
>   though for forty years they saw what I did.
> That is why I was angry with that generation;
>   I said, 'Their hearts are always going astray,
>   and they have not known my ways.'
> So I declared on oath in my anger,
>   'They shall never enter my rest.' "

He further underlines his text, as a good preacher might do, by quoting verse 7-8 ("*Today if you hear his voice, do not harden your hearts*") and verse 11 ("*They shall never enter my rest*") twice more each. He hopes that by doing this, it will *judge the thoughts and attitudes in the hearts of his readers*—both the Hebrews and you.

A Familiar Call to Worship

This text may not seem to you to come from a very familiar Psalm at first glance. But the verses just before the quotation are perhaps the best known of any call to worship in Scripture:

> Come, let us bow down in worship,
>   let us kneel before the LORD our Maker;
> for he is our God
>   and we are the people of his pasture,
>   the flock under his care. (v. 6-7a)

We sing numerous worship songs that echo these words. (You're humming right now, aren't you? Me too...)

What is perhaps interesting in light of the completed work of God that we have been looking at is that the basis of worship in these verses is that he is **our Maker** (his work of creation) and that we are *the flock under his care* (his work of provision). We are called to worship in contemplating the Creator of all and in gratefulness and enjoyment of the way he provides and cares for us. We are reminded that worship is at the heart of rest.

Not only are we to contemplate the Creator, but the first verses of the Psalm remind Israel of God as their Deliverer, the great God of the Exodus, the salvation story of the Old Testament: *Come, let us sing for joy to the LORD; let us shout aloud* **to the Rock of our salvation.** *Let us come before him with thanksgiving and extol him with music and song.* The Rock is a place where the people can feel secure in their deliverance, a place they can rest.

Psalm 62 makes this connection even more explicit:

> Truly **my soul finds rest in God;**
>   *my salvation comes from him.*
> *Truly he is my rock and my salvation;*
>   *he is my fortress, I will never be shaken.* (v. 1-2)

No wonder Psalm 95 invites the people to worship Yahweh with thanksgiving, for their redemption from slavery to be the chosen people of God. What a great reason for praise! In worshipping God for his sure and completed work, we both **state our trust** in him and **find it strengthened**—resulting in deeper rest.

A Stern Warning against Worshiplessness

The part of Psalm 95 that the author of Hebrews quotes, however, is bleaker. It is not a part that we generally include in our worship songs! It is warning of what happens when the Creator and Provider is not acknowledged—when knowledge does not become active belief. The Psalmist reminds them of their forefathers, the ones who had experienced deliverance from slavery, and yet did not trust him when it came to their desert experience. For forty years they had seen what he did—and yet *their hearts went astray.* As Hebrews 4:2 says, "*it was of no value to them.*"

For those who turn away from trust and worship, even after seeing God's goodness and grace—who harden their hearts—rest becomes elusive. Having refused to acknowledge the One whose work is finished, they are left to their own resources, having to provide for themselves and find their own security, identity, purpose—and rest.

No wonder the writer to Hebrews follows his quotation with an injunction: *See to it, brothers, that none of you has a sinful, unbelieving heart that turns away from the living God* (3:12). He knows what restlessness follows.

On the other hand:

- If we are truly resting in our Creator, we will learn to worship him by enjoying him as our Maker and in all he has made.
- If we are resting in God as our Provider, our worship will display itself not only in singing songs, but also in contentment, in gratitude, and in generosity with all he has given us.
- If we are resting in him as Deliverer, we will see him as our Rock, the foundation that cannot be shaken, resulting in joy and thanksgiving.

Encourage One Another in Worship

Hebrews 3:13 tells us a practical way to heed this warning and keep our hearts from getting hard: *But encourage one another daily, as long as it is called Today, so that none of you may be hardened by sin's deceitfulness.* Part of how we do this is in corporate worship together, as we begin to see a new vision of our Father through the words and worship of our brothers and sisters.

We have already seen that when God made the world, he set aside time for rest—and a large part of the rest to which he called us from the beginning was worship of our Creator. We must respond to the Psalmist's call to worship, and heed the warning that he and the writer of Hebrews would give us.

Reflections:

Rest Definition #7:
Rest = worship

- Does this definition seem weird to you? Why or why not? If it does, what do you think you believe (or don't believe) about God that makes worship laborious?
- What happens if you turn this definition around into "worship = resting in God"? How does this idea of line up with the way God made things at the beginning of the world? How does it line up with the way things are headed in eternity future?
- For what are you motivated to worship God right now, in view of his completed works?
    - As Creator
    - As Provider
    - As Redeemer
    - As Restorer
  Think about writing your own "psalm of praise" that would help you state your trust in Him, and find it strengthened.
- What do you think is the value of corporate worship in encouraging faith and resting in God? Can you think of an example of this in your life?

9 Memories of Massah and Meribah

*...**Do not harden your hearts** as you did in the rebellion, during the time of testing in the desert where your fathers tested and tried me and for forty years saw what I did.* (Hebrews 3:8-9)

"Rosebud." The dying Charles Kane gasps out the word with his last breath, in the classic movie *Citizen Kane.* This one word lets loose a flurry of reporters, eager to discover the mystery behind it. Was it a person? A place? What secrets are hidden this one-word utterance? The movie viewers become caught up in the backstory along with the investigating journalist as it unfolds on the silver screen to reveal the answer.

Up to this point in our study of Hebrews 3:7-4:11 there have been questions and mysteries. What is this rebellion? Why was God angry with these people? What was *"the rest"* that they were not able to enter? We come now to that exciting moment in our study where the backstory to the plot is revealed and everything makes sense. Both the writer to the Hebrews and the Psalmist have been referring back to an infamous episode in Israel's history, which you can read below.

Hardness of Heart in Exodus 17:1-7

> The whole Israelite community set out from the Desert of Sin, travelling from place to place as the Lord commanded. They camped at Rephidim, but there was no water for the people to drink. So they quarrelled with Moses and said, "Give us water to drink."
>
> Moses replied, "Why do you quarrel with me? Why do you put the Lord to the test?" But the people were thirsty for water there, and they grumbled against Moses. They said, "Why did you bring us up out of Egypt to make us and our children and livestock die of thirst?" Then Moses cried out to the Lord, "What am I to do with these people? They are almost ready to stone me." The Lord answered Moses, "Walk on ahead of the people. Take with you some of the elders of Israel and take in your hand the staff with which you struck the Nile, and go. I will stand there before you by the rock at Horeb. Strike the rock, and water will come out of it for the people to drink."

So Moses did this in the sight of the elders of Israel. And he called the place Massah [testing] and Meribah [quarrelling] because the Israelites quarrelled and because they tested the Lord saying, "Is the Lord among us or not?"

Before you are too hard on these Israelites, think how anxious about finding water you would be if you had children and livestock to care for, and found yourself with a huge horde of people wandering through the desert. And imagine how taken aback you would find yourself when you reached Rephidim, the fertile oasis of which you had been dreaming for weary miles—only to discover the streams dried up and no way to drink.

In their anxiety and frustration with this situation, the people turn on Moses, accusing him—and thus, indirectly, God—of bringing them out to the desert to die. They quarrel with Moses, and dare God to take care of them, doubting his care and concern: **"Is the Lord among us or not?"** Because of this, the springs that resulted from Moses' striking of the rock at God's command were called Massah, which means "testing," and Meribah, which means "quarrelling." (In the Hebrews version of this Psalm, quoted from the Greek version of the Old Testament called the Septuagint, the writer omits the names and goes straight to their meanings.)

Remembering God's Provision and Deliverance

Anxiety and frustration in this difficult situation are certainly understandable. But on the other hand, just think about some of the things that these people had already seen:

- The plagues on Egypt (seven of which did not affect them, including the death of all firstborn sons)
- The parting of the Red Sea
- The drowning of Pharaoh and his army
- The leading of the cloud and the fire
- The provision of quail and daily manna to eat

You would think that maybe, just maybe, a God who would do all of this for them would not be bringing them out in the desert just to let them die of dehydration! But they could not bring themselves to believe—to rest in knowing that God was leading them and providing for them. They persisted in believing that reality was only what they could see and experience right now.

Because of this kind of hardness of heart, displayed over and over again, God decrees that they will get what they are convinced will happen. They will not "enter the rest" of the Promised Land, the land of provision flowing with milk and honey, the land promised to their ancestors. Rather, they will wander restlessly in the desert until all the adults who had experienced God's deliverance from Egypt are dead.

Hardness of Heart, Take 2

What is **really** sad is that there is another story that is almost an exact replica of this one in Numbers 20.

Once more, there is no water.

Once more they quarrel with Moses, saying, *"Why did you bring the Lord's community into this wilderness, that we and our livestock should die here? Why did you bring us up out of Egypt to this terrible place? It has no grain or figs, grapevines or pomegranates. And there is no water to drink!"* (v. 4-5)

Once more Moses strikes the rock to bring water from it.

And once more the spring, a different one from the last, is called *Meribah* because of their quarrelling and rebellion.

The difference is that it is almost **40 years** later, and these people are the children of those in the Exodus story! Moses says to these people in Deuteronomy 29:2-6: *"Your eyes have seen all that the Lord did in Egypt... With your own eyes you saw those great trials, those signs and great wonders. But to this day the Lord has not given you a mind that understands or eyes that see or ears that hear. Yet the Lord says, 'During the forty years that I led you through the wilderness, your clothes did not wear out, nor did the sandals on your feet... I did this so that you might know that I am the Lord your God.'"*

They have experienced God's provision for them for their whole lives since they were delivered from slavery in Egypt as children—and yet they still are unable to believe that God is trustworthy and faithful, still unable to rest in his wonderful works, his character and his promises.

Don't Let Hard Things Harden You

But before we shake our heads too much at their failure, we must remember how we are tempted to do the same. To see what we are lacking. To focus on our difficult circumstances. To forget God's mercy to us. To let the hard things we face harden our hearts.

The writer to the Hebrews drives home his warning not to make the same mistake by repeating two quotes: *They shall never enter my rest* and *Today, if you hear his voice, **do not harden your hearts.*** He does not want us to make the same mistake. He wants us to remember that even in difficulty, we can rest in God's completed work. And he wants us to hear the voice of God, remembering all that he has done for us, and opening our hearts.

Is the Lord among us, or not? The answer to that question will determine the rest.

Reflections:

- How does this story related to the Psalmist's warning in Psalm 95: that worshiplessness leads to worry and weariness?
- What do you think these two instances (in Exodus and Numbers) say to us about people's tendency to focus on the problems that surround them, rather than recognizing who God is, and what he has done for them?
- What are some of the circumstances that you are facing right now that are causing you stress or anxiety? How are you tempted to react? (Some examples: complaining, taking control, distracting yourself, blaming, manipulating someone else). God does not want you to become hardened in this difficulty! If you wish, write a prayer that expresses your trust in God for this situation.
- Think of someone else who is in difficulty, and encourage them *"while it is Today"*!

Rest Definition #8:
Rest ≠ no difficult circumstances

Rest Definition #9:
Rest = reliance on a loving God who is in control

10 A Desert Lesson in Provision and Rest

*"... Bear in mind that **the LORD has given you the Sabbath**; that is why on the sixth day he gives you bread for two days. Everyone is to stay where he is on the seventh day; no one is to go out."* So the people rested on the seventh day. The people of Israel called the bread manna. It was white like coriander seed and tasted like wafers made with honey. (Exodus 16:29-31)*

*There remains, then, a Sabbath-rest for the people of God; for **anyone who enters God's rest also rests from their works,** just as God did from his. (Hebrews 4:9-10)*

Ladies and gentlemen, let's step into the time machine once again, and go back just a little bit more...

The people's despair about water in Exodus 17 is all the more remarkable when you go back to the previous chapter. (Look up Exodus 16 to read the whole story.) Here, their complaint about God bringing them out in the desert to die is almost identical to that in chapter 17, except they substitute "food" for "water". And they add on a fantasy memory about how good they had it in Egypt—sitting around pots of meat, eating all they wanted... Uh, guys? Don't you remember the slavery? The whips? The backbreaking work?

Nonetheless, God provides for his people: quail in the evening and a "bread from heaven" that the people called "manna" in the morning. This substance coated the ground in the morning and was their primary source of nourishment for the next forty years, never failing to be found and gathered each morning.

Or almost every morning. For God does a strange thing—he uses this new provision as an opportunity to teach his people a little about the value of rest—and what the basis of real rest is.

God as the Source of Provision and Rest

The manna appears six days a week, regular as clockwork. Moses tells the people to gather about an *omer* per person—about 2 quarts (2 litres) each. And as Exodus 16:18 says, with simple eloquence: *And when they measured it by the omer, the one who gathered much did* not have too much, and the one who gathered little did not have too little. Everyone had gathered just as much as they needed.

But some people, of course, get greedy, or afraid that it may not keep coming, or are too lazy to want to gather it every day. So they take more than the recommended amount, and keep it overnight to use the next day. The next morning when they wake up, they ask, "What's that smell?" And they find rotten manna, crawling with manna maggots. Disgusting!

On the sixth day, Moses tells them to gather twice as much as usual, two omers per person. Then he says: "This is what the LORD commanded: 'Tomorrow is to be a day of sabbath rest, a holy sabbath to the LORD. So bake what you want to bake and boil what you want to boil. Save whatever is left and keep it until morning'" (v. 23). And those who follow these instructions discover that the manna that is kept overnight **this** time is still fresh and edible. Delicious!

But some people, of course, know better. They know there is no beating the manna maggots, and that it is up to them to use their common sense and provide for their families. So they get up early on the seventh day to gather their food—and discover that there is none. Because of this, the Lord says to Moses: "How long will these people refuse to obey my commands and instructions? They must realize that **the Sabbath is the Lord's gift to you**" (v. 28-29a, NLT).

God wanted his people to know that the work that they did—gathering the manna—was their part, but that he was the source of provision. He wanted them to know that they safely rest one day each week, knowing that God was taking care of them. **This was his gift to them!** Then they could enjoy what he provided and the rest from their labour, knowing that they did not have to work and worry endlessly. They could offer grateful worship to God, and spend time with each other, and enjoy the bread that he had given them—resting in his presence and provision.

Provision: Our Doing, Or God's?

When you read through this story, do you find yourself getting annoyed at the people who keep doing the opposite of what God says? Like gathering too much manna when they are not supposed to, or trying to go out and gather on the seventh day when God said there wouldn't be any?

But we are just as prone to disbelieve God will provide, to have a hard heart that sees his gifts of provision through our work as our own doing. We work hard, and then we work harder. We think, It is all up to me. We think, How will this get done if I don't do it?

We are also bent towards using our work as a means toward greed, rather than a way of supplying our needs. Or to continue to build up security barriers around ourselves, of finances, and precautions, and "safe" choices. Or to try to make our own kind of rest by stockpiling resources that will allow us to take life easy.

Jesus' parable of the Rich Fool in Luke 12:13-21 tells us how well this works out in the end. The rich man, with his abundant harvest, says to himself, *"You have plenty of grain laid up for many years. Take life easy; eat, drink and be merry."* But God says to him, *"You fool! This very night your life will be demanded from you. Then who will get what you have prepared for yourself?"* Overnight. Maggots. Disgusting.

Trusting in God's Provision of Rest

God's provision for us is not just food and clothes, shelter and companionship, and all else needed for life and health. It also includes the gift of rest—a rest of both body and soul.

He has made it so that we can only truly find this gift in Him. If you turn back to the front of the book, you will find a poem by George Herbert, entitled "The Pulley." (It is a poem worth meditating on.) Herbert's idea is that our need for rest is exactly that—a pulley that draws us back to God when we are heartsick and exhausted, at the end of ourselves. In it God says:

> Yet let [man] keep the rest,
> But keep them with repining restlesnesse:
> Let him be rich and wearie, that at least,
> If goodnesse leade him not, yet wearinesse
> May tosse him to my breast.

The Sabbath was given to the ancient Israelites so that they could rest both body and soul. Body: in forgoing the normal physical work to which God had called them, the daily work of gathering food in a desert. Soul: in spending a day to dedicated to reflection on God and his works, and worshipping him together.

He offers us the same gift, on a daily basis, that he offered them: release from our anxieties and driven-ness through trust and worship, the freedom to physically and regularly stop our work and rest, knowing he is in control. But we are just as liable as they were to reject God's gift of rest, both physically and spiritually. We miss the point that *anyone who enters God's rest **also rests from their works**, just as God did from his* (Heb. 4:10).

God wants us to rely on him both for the provision of our needs, and for the provision of our rest. We can only really rest when we know that it is he that is providing for our needs, and not our personal effort or hoarding. And then we can gratefully accept the gift of time to stop working, to be with him and others, to reflect on all he is, all he has provided for us, to relax and be content in his presence.

Likewise in the spiritual arena, the only good works that count with God are the ones created for you in Christ. Jesus has not just forgiven us, brought us up to zero in our debt to God. He has deposited a vast fortune of righteousness in our accounts, all for us to spend lavishly. When we give up on the effort of proving our own goodness and begin to discover how to disburse the goodness Jesus provides us, the relief is immense!

Why should you rest on your own works, when God offers you the gift of resting in his? Give up your weary works, and open up the package he is holding out to you.

Reflections:

- Think about the Israelites' weird rose-coloured memories of Egypt: *"There we sat around pots of meat and ate all the food we wanted..."* (Ex. 16:3). Isn't it strange how we can get so nostalgic about a past that we have made up—a past that was actually slavery? How we can "horribilize" the situations in which we find ourselves, or the people we are with? How do you see this in yourself?
- We thought earlier about how frustrating it is in the story to see people constantly doing the opposite of God's instructions. How do you see people (or yourself!) doing the same kind of thing when it comes to God's way of resting?
- Meditate for a while on Hebrews 4:9-10: *There remains, then, a Sabbath-rest for the people of God; for anyone who enters God's rest also rests from their works, just as God did from his.* What are the "works" that God is calling you to rest from?
    - Is it working hard to make sure you have enough stuff (whether money or something else) to feel secure?
    - Is it working hard to stockpile enough so that you can "take it easy"? The efforts you expend to create relaxation and pleasure for yourself?
    - Is it working hard to change something you hate about yourself, to live up to an ideal image you have?
    - Is it working hard to look good to others? To have them see you as responsible, or competent, or confident, or admirable in some way? (Or perhaps moral, or spiritual?)
    - Is it working hard to earn God's favour? To show him that you are worthy of his pleasure and blessing? To be as good as, or better than, someone else?

    How, for each of these, would it make a difference to rest in God's works instead? How could you accept his gift?

11 Do not Harden your Hearts

It still remains that some will enter that rest, and those who formerly had the gospel preached to them did not go in, because of their disobedience. Therefore God again set a certain day, calling it Today, when a long time later he spoke through David, as was said before: "Today, if you hear his voice, do not harden your hearts." **For if Joshua had given them rest, God would not have spoken later about another day.** (Hebrews 4:6-8)

Once Dr. Seuss made me cry.

The book that caused the tears was *I Had Trouble Getting to Solla Sollew,* and it told the story of a creature in the Valley of Vung who sets out on a journey to escape his troubles. His destination is Solla Sollew, on the beautiful banks of the river Wah-Hoo, "where they never have troubles—at least very few."

After a stressful journey on which his camel gets the gleeks, suffering attacks by Poozers, and wandering lost for days in tunnels filled with birds going the wrong way, the hero finally reaches his destination. But when he gets there, he discovers that one of the few troubles that they **do** have in Solla Sollew is that a Key-Slapping Slippard has moved into the lock to the gate of the city—and there is no way in. It was at this point that I cried myself to sleep. How could he go through so much to get there, and then not be able to enter? What a tragedy!

The Tragedy of Not Entering God's Rest

The story that we have been looking at from Exodus is an even greater tragedy. These Israelites certainly went through hardship on their way through the desert toward the Promised Land: leaving behind all they had known in Egypt, constantly traveling, having to find food and water, enduring the arid Sinai desert, warding off hostile attackers.

But they also witnessed many miracles of God's care for them: provision of food and water, victory over enemies, even the fact that their clothes and shoes did not wear out (Deuteronomy 8:4). Over and over, God delivered them when their enemies attacked them.

And they experienced many opportunities for repentance and a return to God: after the golden calf, after the infestation of snakes, and many others—times when God forgave their sin and made a way for them to be reconciled to him instead of destroying them.

And yet, when they finally reached the borders of the Promised Land, they could not trust in God enough to believe that he was their Deliverer and Provider in this situation as well. Instead, they fall into a panic as they see the strength of the cities and the size of the inhabitants. Guess what their response is?

> "If only we had died in Egypt! Or in this wilderness! Why is the Lord bringing us to this land only to let us fall by the sword? Our wives and children will be taken as plunder. Wouldn't it be better for us to go back to Egypt?" (Numbers 14:2-3)

Sound like something we have heard before?

Joshua and Caleb, who had been on the scouting party, pleaded with the people: "The land we passed through and explored is exceedingly good. If the Lord is pleased with us, he will lead us into that land, a land flowing with milk and honey, and will give it to us. Only do not rebel against the Lord. And do not be afraid of the people of the land, because we will devour them. Their protection is gone, but **the Lord is with us.** Do not be afraid of them" (Numbers. 14:7-9). But the people just wanted to stone them as dangerously misguided optimists who would get them all killed.

Finally, as the Psalmist says, God declared an oath in [his] anger: "They shall never enter my rest" (Psalm 95:11). Here is the oath: "As for your children that you said would be taken as plunder, I will bring them in to enjoy the land you have rejected. But as for you, **your bodies will fall in this wilderness.** Your children will be shepherds here for forty years, suffering for your unfaithfulness, until the last of your bodies lies in the wilderness" (Numbers 14:31-33).

License: Making My Own Rest instead of Entering His

Tragic. To be at the very border of the Promised Land, and not enter its rest. But this happened because they were more interested in following their own way, even if it meant the golden calf and debauchery. More concerned about finding their own rest, even if it meant going back to slavery. More focused on doing as they wished.

At first glance, "doing whatever I want to do" sounds like a good definition of rest. Isn't this what we mean when we talk about "leisure time"? The time to indulge in whatever I choose?

There is a slippery slope here. It is good to have choices, to have space, to participate in recreational activities. But the subtle temptation to let **my** desires, **my** choices be the ruling factor in how I rest can lead to hardness of heart. And as a result, we can end up on the other side of the fence, always chasing rest and never achieving it, as the ancient Israelites did. (We will consider this in more detail in a later chapter.)

Legalism: Resting on My Own Works Instead of His

The writer to the Hebrews presses home this point to his audience by quoting this verse twice: *They shall never enter my rest.* He was speaking to people who were, like their forefathers, in a difficult and dangerous situation. There was plenty to make them anxious as they underwent persecution from their fellow Jews after having converted to Christianity. Having experienced the grace of the Messiah, Jesus, they were now in danger of turning back to the legalistic system of first-century Judaism because of lost jobs, economic difficulty and severe social pressure. Just as their forefathers had tasted God's goodness and still failed to trust in the face of difficulties, these people were on the verge of failing to enter God's rest in the completed work of the Messiah.

Instead of trusting in the finished work of Jesus, they were tempted to trust their own righteous rule-keeping, as they rigidly followed not only the laws of the Old Testament, but all of the legalistic rules that had been set up as a "fence" around the law. The writer does not imply that God's law is bad, but rather that it cannot, by itself, bring them into right relationship with God:

> The law is only a shadow of the good things that are coming—not the realities themselves. For this reason it can never, by the same sacrifices repeated endlessly year after year, make perfect those who draw near to worship (Hebrews 10:1).

He paints a picture that this sin of turning away from *the gospel preached to them* is in fact even worse than their ancestors' sin:
Anyone who rejected the law of Moses died without mercy on the testimony of two or three witnesses. How much more severely do you think someone deserves to be punished who has trampled the Son of

God underfoot, who has treated as an unholy thing the blood of the covenant that sanctified them, and who has insulted the Spirit of grace? (Hebrews 10:28-29)

He urges them strongly to change their perspective right away—"Today", as the Psalmist says. He argues that the physical rest of God's people in the Promised Land was only a foreshadowing of the spiritual rest that they would be given through the Promised One. Many of their fellow Jews, like their forefathers, continued to resist the deliverance and provision of God that had been made for them in the Messiah, Jesus—and he does not want them to make that same mistake.

Rejecting Our Self-Made Rest and Works for God's

The Old Testament Israelites wanted it easy—rest on their own terms. They wanted to do what they wanted to do when they wanted it—a way of thinking we could call **"license."**

The New Testament Jews were more drawn to **"legalism"**—the idea of working in one's own strength to prove "good enough" to God, through obedience to a standard of perfection.

These options are also available to us *Today*. But we also have the option, by faith, of trusting in God's completed works, and of finding a Sabbath rest better than that of the Promised Land. Don't put off believing—delay hardens the heart.

Reflections:

- **License** is the mind-set that I should do what I want to do however and whenever I want to do it. How is this evidence of disbelief and a "hard heart"?
- It seems on the surface that "doing whatever I want to do" would be a good definition of rest. What are the dangers and limitations of this definition?
- **Legalism** is the belief that I can be righteous through my own actions, through obeying the rules, and through being better than others. How is this an antidote to rest? How is it evidence of disbelief and a "hard heart"?
- Why are we attracted to legalism? What does it appear to satisfy in us?

Rest Definition #10:
Rest ≠ doing whatever you want

Rest Definition #11:
Rest ≠ achieving spiritual perfection

12 A Symphony of Sabbath

*For if Joshua had given them rest, God would not have spoken later about another day. There remains, then, **a Sabbath-rest for the people of God**; for anyone who enters God's rest also rests from his own work, just as God did from his.* (Hebrews 4:8-10)

Have you ever listened to a Renaissance madrigal? Each voice in the music is singing its own melody, but it is as these parts are put together and create harmony that the magic happens—the individual voices and parts creating a complete picture.

The theologian N.T. Wright suggests that we can read Scripture this way, as though there were different voices running through it that must be harmonized and heard together, and yet have distinct parts. As we have been looking at Hebrews 3 & 4, we can distinguish at least six different parts that are being sung. And in doing so, we get a much fuller picture of what it means that *there remains a Sabbath-rest for the people of God.*[*]

The Bass and Baritone lines

The foundational part, the bass line, comes from the character of God and his story of love for his creation from the beginning of the world. The meaning of the first Sabbath was that God had finished his work of creation. All was made that would be made. Now God would provide for that creation, and his care was as sure as the creation was complete. His creatures could rest in knowing that their Maker was caring for them and providing for them—and they could even rest from their work of taking care of creation one day a week, knowing their efforts were not the primary factor in the equation of met needs.

Of course, when we think of the Sabbath, many of us picture a Jewish celebration, with families lighting candles and eating a meal. The Old Testament nation of Israel has the baritone part in this piece of Scriptural music, both the discordant notes of the hard-hearted people in the desert and the sweet tones of the Psalmist who calls to

---

[*] I am indebted to my husband, Carlton Deal, for his adaptation of N.T. Wright's metaphor from *The Cross and The Colliery* to this text.

them to worship, with a warning. God gave them the Sabbath so that they would have the time not just to exist, but to really live, as they declared weekly their dependence on him by refraining from work, resting along with their households, and reflecting on the God who sustained and delivered them.

The Melody and Tenor Lines

But the melody line in this madrigal—the sweetest and most important part—is sung by Jesus. It is he through whom God spoke to us in these last days (Hebrews 1:2), and through whom God not only created, but re-created the world by his death, resurrection and ascension.

In this new-creation Sabbath-rest, God's children could know that they had been re-made by his hand—fully and completely. They were reconciled with the Father, released from the penalty of sin, and redeemed to be his dearly loved sons and daughters. Now Jesus would perfect those he had redeemed, and his gradual sculpting of them into his own image was just as sure as the work of redemption was complete. God's children could rest in knowing that their Redeemer was bringing out the masterpiece that he had created them to be. They could *"rest from their own work"* as they trusted Christ's perfect righteousness to be their record, and his death as their atonement for sin. As they *fix their eyes on Jesus, the pioneer and perfecter of our faith*, they gain strength so they will not grow weary and lose heart (Hebrews 12:2-3).

The tenor part, sung by the Church from the time of the Hebrews letter till now, echoes this stirring melody. In spite of all that she has faced in persecution, in spite of heresy and rationalism and materialism, the Church has always found a Sabbath-rest in their faith in Jesus—a *confidence in what we hope for and assurance about what we do not see* (Hebrews 11:1). Even in the midst of difficult circumstances, the Bride and Body of Christ, of whom we are members, can *hold unswervingly to the hope we profess, for he who promised is faithful* (Hebrews 10:23).

The Descant Line

And one reason we can sing this tune is because, high above them, is a descant to the melody that soars with wonder and promise, sung by the Spirit of God. For the Promised Land into which Joshua eventually led the children of Israel is nothing compared with what is coming when God's restoration is finally complete. As the writer to the Hebrews says, in exhorting his friends not to be afraid of bearing disgrace for Jesus' name: *For here we do not have an enduring city, but we are looking for the city that is to come* (Hebrews 13:14). This will be the ultimate Sabbath-rest—to dwell in the New Creation:

> *Then the angel showed me the river of the water of life, as clear as crystal, flowing... down the middle of the great street of the city. On each side of the river stood the tree of life... And the leaves of the tree are for the healing of the nations. No longer will there be any curse. The throne of God and of the Lamb will be in the city, and his servants will serve him... They will not need the light of a lamp or the light of the sun, for the Lord God will give them light. And they will reign forever and ever* (Revelation 22:1-5, selected).

One of the fears people sometimes have about eternal life in this City of God is boredom. Do we really want to rest and do nothing through all eternity? (Except for maybe harp lessons?) But it seems clear in this text that there will be activity—even work—in this New Creation. Why else would it say that *his servants will **serve** him*? Or that *they will **reign*** for ever and ever? Sounds a lot like work to me!

Part of our problem here is that we define rest as "doing nothing." Sometimes there is nothing more tiring than doing nothing. This is one explanation for why we find this conventional picture of heaven so unappealing. Another is that we cannot imagine what it will be like to be able to rest and work simultaneously, as we will be able to in eternity. We will be made more like God, who is both Eternal Work and Eternal Rest. So our work will not be tiring, and our rest will not be boring.

Your Part in the Sabbath Song

Fortunately, we get to practice a bit for this kind of Sabbath-rest even while we are here in this present time—by resting in God through faith, even when tired, even while working, even in the midst of difficulty. And that is where the alto line of the song of Hebrews 3&4 comes in—you are the one who gets to sing it! You have the opportunity to harmonize with this great Song of Rest, sung by the Triune God along with his people throughout the ages. You have the chance to sing Sabbath in your own life and experience.

Here is a full-circle picture of the Sabbath-rest of God following the creation of the world, and the rest that you are invited into for eternity as God re-creates the heavens and the earth. You are offered rest in every area of your life, and it begins with what you believe about God.

"Today, if you hear his voice,
do not harden your heart."

Is he your Creator? He will care for you—you do not have to be consumed with anxiety, no matter what is happening to you. Is he the Father to whom you have been reconciled by Jesus? He will live in you and make you more and more like his Son—you can rest in his love, no matter who or what you are up against.

As you sing your part in this song of faith, you will come closer to entering his rest—first in your mind and heart, and then as this rest is reflected in your lifestyle. And your song will *encourage others as long as it is called "Today," so that none of you may be hardened by sin's deceitfulness.*

Reflections:

- Does it help you to see these different parts of the harmony? In what ways? How might having a full-circle picture of rest from the beginning of Creation into eternity future, and encompassing the people of God throughout time, give you perspective on the rest that you are offered in Jesus?
- How did the description of the City of God fit with the image you have of heaven? How much of your image of heaven seems boring because it involves doing nothing? How does it help you to think of a new creation in which your work is not tiring, and your rest is not boring—where in fact you will be able to rest and work simultaneously?
- Think about what beliefs you may have that are blocking you from entering God's rest, just as we did earlier with the characters from the introduction. Take some time to do this, prayerfully reflecting on your own life and behaviour, your emotions and desires, your physical state and spiritual attitudes. (Hint: look for areas of anxiety and exhaustion, some of the symptoms you might have identified in the first chapter.) What do you need to believe differently about God, in order to combat *hardness of heart* and *enter his rest*? How can you begin to do that, *Today*?

part three:
creating containers
for rest

13 Making Efforts to Enter Rest

*Let us, therefore, **make every effort to enter that rest,** so that no one will fall by following their example of disobedience.* (Hebrews 4:11)

It strikes me me as paradoxical that this verse tells us that we must **make an effort** to enter rest! Aren't *effort* and *rest* opposites?

But the thing that comes easy to us is self-dependence. Left to ourselves, we will naturally think that we are in charge of our own lives—and then discover that it is a burdensome responsibility. How much stuff is enough? Enough to be secure? Enough to be important? And what is the role of our work? To define who we are? To fulfil us? To simply earn enough money to be able to retire and/or play?

And this is only the personal part of self-dependence, not even the spiritual part of it. When are we good enough? How many good things do we have to do to be good enough? How do I even decide what is good and what is not? Most religions are formed to try to answer just these questions and build a spiritual ladder that one can climb towards peace and perfection.

Efforts to Resist Self-Dependence

This self-dependence—or, as the Hebrews passage terms it, *hardness of heart* or *disobedience*—is what we must make the effort to resist if we are to enter into rest. Instead, we must keep picking up our reliance and squarely putting it back on the One who is really in control, the only One to whom we can give the steering wheel in safety and relax.

We do this firstly, as we have already seen, by believing—really believing, in a way that makes a difference to what we do—in God's work on our behalf. We trust that he will provide for all of our needs just as surely as he is our Creator. And we trust that he will continue to work in and through us, just as surely as he has reconciled us to himself through the gift of his Son.

This kind of effort is what the writer to the Hebrews was talking about in these verses: *We want each of you to show this same diligence to the very end, so that what you hope for may be fully realized. We do not want you to become lazy, but to imitate those who through faith and patience inherit what has been promised.* (Hebrews 6:11-12)

But the second way we do this is by acting on this belief in practical ways. One way that we can show this diligence is to cultivate healthy and Biblical work practices and rest rhythms. Another is by creating disciplines of rest that act as checkpoints for us in our efforts to truly enter his rest.

Creating Containers for Rest

Think of those little plastic containers that you use to put your leftovers into the fridge. Imagine what it would be like if you just dumped your leftover Kung Pao Chicken directly onto the refrigerator shelf with no container. Now imagine if **none** of the food in your fridge was in a container! What a mess!

These practices and disciplines are like containers—they help to keep our lives from becoming jumbled and mixed together. The Sabbath was a container that helped the Jewish people to differentiate between work and rest, and to carve out a focused respite that would enable them to work out of that rest. God gave the people of Israel (and us) six containers—also known as "days"—that were supposed to be largely filled with work, and one container that was supposed to be reserved for rest.

Without disciplines of rest, we run the danger of robbing ourselves of the rest experience that God would have for us in our everyday lives. If we feel that the world (at least our personal world) depends upon our work, then we will work more or less constantly unless constrained to stop by exhaustion or sickness. There is no container for our work, and so it just bleeds into everything.

It takes a little extra effort to put things into containers, instead of just dumping them wherever. But the mess that is avoided…

The Container vs. The Contents

Now think again about your little plastic containers, full of food in your fridge. Nice and neat. Here's the question: what is more important—the container or what it contains? What if you tipped the food into the trash and put the container on your plate instead?

Here's another danger: focusing on the container rather than the contents—that is, concentrating our effort on the **discipline** of rest rather than *making every effort to enter God's rest.*

One problem with the first-century Jews was that they had stopped focusing as much on the contents of the container (enjoying God, others, and his creation) and had become focused on the container itself (the Sabbath laws). These had become more and more strict as the observance of Sabbath became in itself a work that demonstrated one's holiness and acceptability to God. The Sabbath had become a chance to **demonstrate** self-reliance, rather than an opportunity to turn from it.

We can do this same thing if we become **focused on disciplines rather than the rest they are meant to provide.**

Think of poor Alice the artist in our introduction, who spends a good bit of each of her "quiet times" grovelling before God for not having had enough quiet times. Talk about self-defeating! The purpose of enjoying time with God is tainted by the focus on the acceptability of her "quiet time" container, and the frequency of its use.

Another way that we do this is making our schedule the starting point for rest (or our diet or our sleep...) rather than starting with our hearts. We think that just making time for rest ensures that real rest will occur, not realizing that without resting first in Christ our rest will be unproductive. Discipline in itself is never enough, but is only a container that we fill with **real** rest.

Filling the Containers with Real Rest

Another problem with containers is that we sometimes fill them with the wrong things. I once poured myself a nice big glass of what I thought was apple juice—but was actually recycled oil from a deep fat fryer I had put into an apple juice bottle! We can sometimes try to create space for rest, but then fill it with things that actually rob us of rest instead.

Think of Phoebe, who collapses in exhaustion each day in front of the TV with a glass of wine. Or Bill, who fills all his spare time (and some of his work hours) with football. These strategies are meant as a respite, an escape from the stress of life and work—and in smallish doses, done in a spirit of thankfulness to God, they can be helpful. But like an addict turning to ever-higher doses to get the required kick, Bill and Phoebe will find eventually that the pleasure diminishes with overuse, and discover an emptiness that is equally exhausting. If we rely on ourselves to create our own rest, we will invariably fill the containers with things as unsatisfying to our thirst as used frying oil on a hot day.

Overflowing the Containers

A final problem with containers is that sometimes things are **supposed** to be mixed! Not everything is meant to be totally compartmentalized. The Sabbath practice of spending time focused on God is not meant to be restricted to the Sabbath, but to give us an experience that can overflow into all of our times. We can experience God's rest in our daily lives as we allow our worship of God and fellowship with others to inform the way we live, in glorifying and enjoying him.

This is a tough balance. It is an effort. We would like to rely on ourselves to make our own rest, to carve out time to be selfish and to refuel ourselves according to our own appetites. We would like to call attention to our disciplines of rest rather than their contents— perhaps so that the rest of our time can be called "our own." It takes an effort to enter the rest that God has made for us—to seek out all the ways that God calls us to rest. But this effort is worth it. Rest assured.

Reflections:

Rest Definition # 12:
Rest ≠ no effort

- How does self-reliance manifest itself in you? In the way you pursue your career? In the way you accept (or fail to accept) help from others? In the way you develop relationships? In the way you set goals? In the way you spend your free time? In the efforts you make to be a good person?
- What are the advantages of cultivating spiritual disciplines (regular prayer times, observing a day of rest, Bible study and/or meditation, spiritual retreats, and so on) in helping one to enter the kind of rest we have been talking about? In helping to beat back self-reliance?
- Which of the dangers described do you think you would need to watch out for in using these disciplines? Why would this be a tendency for you?
    - No containers?
    - Making the container more important than the contents?
    - Filling the containers with the wrong things?
    - Or being too compartmentalised?
- Where do you see yourself needing practical help in creating good rhythms of rest and/or spiritual disciplines of rest? Who could be your partner(s) in this?

14 The Rhythm of Rest

*"**Remember the Sabbath day by keeping it holy.** Six days you shall labour and do all your work, but the seventh day is a Sabbath to the Lord your God. On it you shall not do any work, neither you, nor your son or daughter, nor your manservant or maidservant, nor your animals, nor the alien within your gates. For in six days the Lord made the heavens and the earth, the sea, and all that is in them, but he rested on the seventh day. Therefore the Lord blessed the Sabbath day and made it holy."* (Exodus 2:8-11)

Up to now, our discussion of rest has been more theological and spiritual than practical. While we start with a heart of faith that rests in God, he has also made us with bodies that need rest! Fortunately, God has given us many practical directives in **how** to rest—the most prominent one being the Fourth of the Ten Commandments.

The Neglected Commandment

It is a curious thing to consider this fourth commandment. All the commandments following this one are widely acknowledged by almost everyone in the world as a good idea: honouring parents, no murder, no adultery, no stealing, no lying, no envy... And most Christians would consider the first three Commandments, about worshipping only God and keeping his name holy, as of extreme importance.

So why do most people act like this one has been repealed? Especially when, as we have seen, this was not just a Jewish custom, but an ordinance dating from the very creation of the world?

Observing weekly times of rest is not just a good idea—it is a need. This is a rhythm that has been hardwired into us physically, and we ignore it to the detriment of our health and sanity, as much as if we gave up sleeping.

But stopping work for a day was not the only thing that made Sabbath restful. The Israelites were told to *remember the Sabbath day by keeping it holy.* "Holy" means "set apart"—it was a day that is different than other days because it was a day for reflection and relationship. It was a day to reconnect with the Creator and his creation. It was a day to let go of the worries and the drives of the week, and to remember who really is the Source of every blessing. It was a day for being rather than doing, for enjoying God and other people.

It is interesting to notice that while the Exodus version of the commandments (at the beginning of this chapter) cites the Creation basis for the Sabbath, the Deuteronomy version has a different foundation: *Remember that you were slaves in Egypt and that the Lord your God brought you out of there with a mighty hand and an outstretched arm. Therefore the Lord your God has commanded you to observe the Sabbath day* (5:15).

A slave cannot choose when to work and when to rest, but must work whenever the master commands. Thus it was also a day to remember the one who had freed them from slavery in Egypt, and had called them to be his chosen people. It was a day to remember his grace and rejoice in their deliverance and freedom.

Learning From the Hebrew Sabbath

The writer of the Hebrews spends a great deal of time in his book explaining how Old Testament rules and customs help to picture the realities of the New Covenant. Thus, even though under this New Covenant we are not bound by details of the Mosaic Sabbath laws, there is much that we can learn from them. Here are a few things to notice about the Sabbath commands in the Old Testament:

First, God wasn't messing around with this one. He thinks it is really, really, **really** important to rest. Under Mosaic law, a person who desecrated the Sabbath could be put to death, and a person who worked on the Sabbath could be banished (Exodus 31:14). This may seem just a little harsh to us (as probably none of us would be alive), but it shows just how seriously God wanted this command to be taken—as strongly as the law against murder. Which makes it all the more amazing that this is the Commandment we think of as "optional."

Another thing to notice is that no one had more right to rest than anyone else. On the Sabbath, not only the householder was supposed to rest, but everyone in the house, including children, servants and animals. Deuteronomy 5:14 makes this even more explicit, by saying, *so that your male and female servants may rest, as you do.* It is then that he goes on to say, *Remember that you were slaves in Egypt...*

The idea that "leisure" is a privilege of the wealthy is wrong, and we would all agree with that—on the surface. But the way people work to be wealthy enough to have other people do their work for them shows that this is often just lip service to political correctness. In God's economy, everyone is equally required to both work and rest, and the "master"—the head of household or employer—was responsible to make sure that those who worked for him also had their day of rest.

Chick-Fil-A, a fast food restaurant chain in the US that was started by Christians, has attempted to take this idea to heart in our day. In a country where many conveniences are open 24/7, they close on Sunday to allow **all** of their employees, managers and servers alike, to have a day of rest. What a counter-cultural move in a competitive business where profits usually rule!

Sabbath Observance vs. Sabbath Attitude

A final note about the Old Testament Sabbath is this: even then, God cared way more about a Sabbath attitude than a Sabbath observance. Just keeping the Sabbath ritual was not enough. In fact, this could become just one more part of self-reliance—and thus something God hates:

> Stop bringing meaningless offerings!
>   Your incense is detestable to me.
> New Moons, Sabbaths and convocations—
>   I cannot bear your worthless assemblies...
> They have become a burden to me;
>   I am weary of bearing them. (Isaiah 1:12-14)

This is a picture of people who are observing the Sabbath, but with the same kind of *hardness of heart* that we observed in the desert Israelites. They do what they wish, cheating people and enriching themselves, and then throw God a pious bone by following the Sabbath ritual, a legalistic self-justification.

But God cannot stand this kind of hypocrisy. What he wants are people who are repentant, seeking his ways in their daily life and resting in him for redemption and renewal. Then, as they take the time on one day a week to rest in him and enjoy his presence, they will experience the essence of a true Sabbath:

"If you keep your feet from breaking the Sabbath
and from doing as you please on my holy day,
if you call the Sabbath a delight
and the Lord's holy day honourable,
and if you honour it by not going your own way
and not doing as you please or speaking idle words,
then you will find your joy in the Lord...*"* (Isaiah 58:13-14).

This is as much a need for us as it was in Old Testament times. It is not enough for us to just stop work for a day and do whatever we want. We have also been made with needs of time for reflection and relationship, for worship and gratitude, for family and friendship. And while our rules for observing the Sabbath may have changed since ancient times, God's heart for us to actually **spend time** resting in him has not.

Reflections:

Rest Definition #13:
Rest = spending time dedicated to God

Rest Definition #14:
Rest = reflection and reconnection

- Why do you think people consider the Fourth Commandment less important than the rest? What do you think its place in this particular list might say about its importance?
- Do you take a day off of your regular work every week? Why or why not? What activities does it usually include?
- What physical symptoms do you experience when you are not resting enough or are working too much?
- What spiritual symptoms do we experience when we are not making time for reflection and relationship, for worship and gratitude, for family and friendship, or when we are resting only in self-centred ways?
- What are some ways that we, like the ancient Israelites, could centre a day of rest on God's grace and provision?

15 A Sabbath for Our Benefit

*One Sabbath Jesus was going through the grain fields, and as his disciples walked along, they began to pick some heads of grain. The Pharisees said to him, "Look, why are they doing what is unlawful on the Sabbath?" (...) Then [Jesus] said to them, "**The Sabbath was made for man, not man for the Sabbath.** So the Son of Man is Lord even of the Sabbath."* (Mark 2:23-24, 27-28)

What did Jesus, often condemned by the Pharisees as a Sabbath-breaker, think about this law and custom? Did he discredit it as of no importance in his life and ministry?

At the end of Mark 2 and the beginning of Mark 3, there are two little stories about Jesus and the Sabbath. (Go ahead—look them up!) In the first, excerpted above, Jesus and his disciples are criticized by the Pharisees for having picked and eaten some grain as they went along. As itinerant wanderers, they were poor and were allowed to glean from the edges of the fields to feed themselves. But this action, to the Pharisees, was considered "reaping" and therefore unlawful. Jesus counters their criticism with a reference to David's eating the consecrated bread from the Tabernacle when he was fleeing from Saul. What has more importance, he asks—"holiness" or hunger?

In the second story, Jesus heals a man with an atrophied hand on the Sabbath. Again, the Pharisees are watching for the chance to accuse this rabbi as a Sabbath-breaker. (Remember, there were serious consequences for this in Old Testament law!) But Jesus sees their *stubborn hearts*, and asks them: What has more importance—"holiness" or healing?

Did Jesus care about the Sabbath? Maybe at first glance these two little stories make it appear that he did not—that the Sabbath was now as passé in his new order as kosher laws later would be. After all, he directly goes against the prevailing Sabbath rules of the day by picking and eating food on the Sabbath. And when it comes to healing, it can seem from reading the Gospels that he went out of his way to perform these miracles on the Sabbath! (See Luke 14:1-6; John 5:1-14; and John 9:1-16 for further examples.)

Works of Necessity and Mercy

Many theologians have commented that what Jesus was actually doing was pointing out the exceptions that had always existed to the Sabbath rules: works of necessity and mercy.

Works of necessity are such things as feeding oneself. Should Jesus and his disciples have gone hungry just to avoid the act of picking some heads of grain? There are many works of necessity that may need to be done on a day of rest: cooking, taking care of children, changing a flat tire, and so on. These may not only be our own necessities, but also a response to the necessities of others around us. When the day your neighbour must move house is Sunday, rolling up your sleeves and carting out boxes is an appropriate activity, even if that is your usual day of rest.

Works of mercy are things that alleviate the sufferings of others—both animals and humans. When in Luke 13 Jesus was criticized for healing on the Sabbath a woman who had been completely crippled by a spirit for eighteen years, he says to his critics, *"You hypocrites! Doesn't each of you on the Sabbath untie your ox or donkey from the stall and lead it out to give it water? Then should not this woman, a daughter of Abraham, whom Satan has kept bound for eighteen long years, be set free on the Sabbath day from what bound her?"* (v. 15-16)

In each of these cases, Jesus was showing how the Pharisees had perverted the Sabbath by making it all about the rules and forgetting about the people. They were focusing on the container and forgetting all about the contents—the requirements of God to *act justly, love mercy, and walk humbly with their God* (Micah 6:8). Jesus showed up their "holiness" for hard-heartedness, and made the Sabbath human again.

A True Sabbath Spirit: Provision and Restoration

Jesus had the right to demonstrate what Sabbath really was about because of his relationship with the Father. In Jewish tradition, the only Person who had the right to work on the Sabbath was God himself. But when Jesus is accused of breaking the Sabbath after healing the man by the pool in John 5, he replies to his accusers, *"My Father is always at his work to this very day, and I too am working"* (5:17). It is not only because he calls God his Father here that his hearers understand these words as a claim to be God, but also that he claims to be **above** Sabbath, with the right to define it, which he could do only as part of the Godhead that is both Eternal Work and Eternal Rest.

This Lordship of Jesus over the Sabbath encourages us to look even more closely at what he was doing in Mark 2 & 3. Rather than allowing his disciples to go hungry, he encouraged them to take advantage of the provision of God for their needs along the way. This went along with a true Sabbath spirit that rests in God as the Provider of all. And in his work of mercy to this poor crippled man, he demonstrates the grace that he would later offer to all on the cross—the chance to be restored and be made whole. Once again, the true spirit of Sabbath is demonstrated as the grace of God becomes the foundation of rest.

As we noted previously, the contents are more important than the container is. The Sabbath is a discipline, valuable because it helps people to stop and reflect. It is a concrete way to put into practice God's invitation to *"Be still and know that I am God"* (Psalm 46:10). As such, it is a gift from God to man, not a rule by which God judges our righteousness. As Lord of the Sabbath, Jesus was inviting us to into a relationship with him that would bring this gift into our everyday lives, rather than simply imposing a religious ritual blindly followed.

Observing Sabbath in Our Day

We can continue to practice the discipline of Sabbath times—a day a week, a time each day, extended retreats—in this spirit of receiving a gift, of enjoying our Creator and Redeemer. It's not about impressing God with our piety, but stopping to be impressed by Him.

However, we must not do this in the spirit of the Pharisees that Jesus opposed, as a legalistic following of rules. Rather, we do it by choice and as a prophetic sign of the New Creation, of the day when our rest will be perfect in the City of God. Paul writes in Colossians 2:16-17: *"Therefore do not let anyone judge you by what you eat or drink, or with regard to a religious festival, a New Moon celebration or a Sabbath day.* ***These are a shadow of the things that were to come; the reality, however, is found in Christ.****"* It is in Christ that our real rest—the rest of faith in his finished work—is found, not in pious observance of detailed decrees. He is the substance behind the shadow.

So how do we practice Sabbath in our day? Most Christians no longer observe a seventh-day Sabbath; those who do observe a weekly Sabbath usually do so on Sunday—the Eighth Day of the Risen Son, the day he initiated his New Creation.

Others say it is the **principle** of the Sabbath—resting and reflecting one day in seven—that is important. Indeed, for some people (such as pastors!) it is not possible for them to abstain from their regular job on a Sunday, because they are involved with works of necessity, mercy, or ministry. They might choose another day, or a large part of a day, to dedicate to God as a focused time for rest and contemplation. It is also worthwhile to extend Sabbath times into the daily schedule with regular times of prayer and meditation, Bible study with others, and so on.

Jesus, having fulfilled the Law, declares that *Sabbath was made for man*. Why should we not avail ourselves of this blessing given to us by God for our benefit? The Sabbath day was created by God as a container to set aside time to worship God and be with our family and his people. It allows for necessary work that meets our needs and the needs of others with thanks for God's provision. And it looks for opportunities to alleviate misery in those around us, extending God's mercy. The Sabbath is not meant to be a chore, but a joy—part of the fulfilment of being the whole person God wants us to be.

And as Jesus also reminds us in his declaration, it is God who made the Sabbath, and it is a reminder that all time is his—that he is the Author of Time. When we dedicate Sabbath times to him, whether a half-hour, a day, or a week, we are reminded that the same dependence and enjoyment of him that are deliberately cultivated in this discipline are possible in **all** of our time, whether work or leisure.

In these Sabbath times, we can renounce self-reliance and reset our centre, reminding ourselves in practical, physical, relational ways of the spiritual rest that Jesus promises is available to us in every day. And we can prophetically foreshadow life in the City of God, in his New Creation, when we will be at rest even while serving God in a joyful eternity. By doing this, the rest that we experience in these times can overflow the containers and colour the rest of our days with peace and freedom.

Reflections:

- What connections do you see between resting in God's provision and renewal, and observing Sabbath times? How does using Sabbath containers affirm our trust in God for these works, and our celebration of them?
- Prayerfully meditate on your usual weekly schedule. How can you accept this practical gift of rest that God is offering you? What Sabbath times do you already have in your life? Are there any other times that you would like to add or try?
- Are you the kind of person who easily falls into a "follow the rules" mentality? If so, how can you guard against this tendency in receiving Sabbath times as a gift?
- Think about Sunday, the traditional Christian Sabbath. Does the way you spend this day lend itself to rest? Is this a good day for you to set aside as a Sabbath time, due to fewer pressures from your everyday work? Or are there necessary responsibilities on that day that would lead you to set aside another day or portion of time to rest fully? (You might also want to evaluate whether activities you think of as necessary truly are...)
- What kind of effort do you think God would want you to make in carving out Sabbath time in your life? What are some of the important aspects of Sabbath rest that you think you might tend to overlook?

Rest definition #15:
Rest = a gift from God

16 Don't Give Up Meeting Together

*And let us consider **how we may spur one another on toward love and good deeds, not giving up meeting together,** as some are in the habit of doing, but encouraging one another—and all the more as you see the Day approaching.* (Hebrews 10:24-25)

Let's face it—church can be complicated! And going can feel more like a chore than a rest, especially after you've gotten all ready to go and Jimmy suddenly throws up on his Sunday shirt... Sometimes it feels like we could rest better if we were just alone in the woods with God and the birds. It's not surprising that regular church attendance among western Christians is at an all time low.

But just as our rest isn't meant to be selfish, it also isn't meant to be completely solitary. True, there are days and hours when a silent retreat or meditation by a lake is what is called for. But the writer to the Hebrews, in encouraging us to *make an effort to enter God's rest,* also exhorts us to *not giving up meeting together, as some are in the habit of doing.*

Don't Give Up Meeting Together

Of course, the reasons that the Hebrews were avoiding gathering together were a bit more serious than ours. They were in danger of being identified with a renegade group and marked out for persecution, losing their homes and livelihoods. For us, the reason is more likely to be that we want to get a bit of extra sleep. Or because the kids have an away game that day.

This is not to say that the church is all about meetings. However, without regularly scheduled times to gather together, we can become isolated, no longer connected to the Body of Christ. And we do this on a Sunday, the traditional Christian Sabbath, for a reason. It is a common container into which we can pour our communal worship, and through which we are mutually encouraged to rest in Christ in a deeper way.

But even when we do go, we can make church more about the container than about what it contains. It becomes a bone we throw to God, just as the Israelites did with the Sabbath in Isaiah's day. We go so that God will get off our backs the rest of the week after we have done our religious duty.

Cutting Consumer Churchgoing

More subtle, and perhaps more common among regular churchgoers is a sense that church is all about me, a commodity that I consume. Did I enjoy the music today? Do I feel "fed" by the pastor's messages? How do my teenagers like the youth ministry? This is another case of putting the wrong things into the container, as though church were a fast-food joint where I stuff in as many spiritual calories as possible before rushing out the door.

Perhaps this is one of the big reasons why "going to church" is so tiring—because it is about image, and duty, and "getting something out of it." We come and sit with dozens or hundreds or thousands of people, never really exchanging any more than pleasantries, and never really connecting with the real Body of Christ, instead of being encouraged by each other and gaining strength and rest to carry out the good works that God has called us to do.

Notice in the text at the beginning of the chapter that the writer of the Hebrews did not say, "And let us consider how **the pastor** can spur us on to love and good deeds..." And yet that is precisely what happens when many churches *meet together.* There is no sense of this kind of strengthening being something that we do for *one another.*

How could this be different? Some smaller churches (house churches, for example) include discussion as a part of the gathering. This does not preclude prepared teaching—in fact, it is far better if discussion is a reaction to a well-thought-through exposition and carefully crafted questions rather than just opening the Bible and saying, "What does this mean to you?" (This latter approach usually opens the doors to a pooling of ignorance rather than to a vigorous interaction with Scripture.)

But even in bigger churches, there are smaller forums such as Sunday School classes and home groups. It would also be possible after a large gathering for a small group of people to go out or to a home for a meal or a drink. Or perhaps we could even make it into a weekly small group on a Sunday night. Then we could really try to wrestle with and apply the text and its message (rather than dissect whether we "liked" the teacher or not).

Acting as Priests to One Another

I Peter 2:5 says: *You also, like living stones, are being built into a spiritual house to be a holy priesthood, offering spiritual sacrifices acceptable to God through Jesus Christ.* Each of us, no matter how young or old, no matter if we came to Christ this year or 30 years ago, is a priest before God, able to enter God's presence. And because of this, we each are able to bring each other before God as well, to strengthen each other, and further his re-creation of us as individuals and as a Body.

I experienced this a number of years ago when teaching children in our international church in Geneva, Switzerland. Many times their insights into Biblical truth were at the same time simple and profound and moved me greatly, and I would walk out of a lesson I had written with a deeper understanding because of their interaction. One time as I told the story of the Giving of the Law on Mount Sinai, I described to the class how the people trembled with fear before the mountain. One little blonde five-year-old girl said, "But don't they know that they should *cast all their anxiety on Him, because he cares for them?*" Bravo. In a few words, she applied much of what I have been writing about for the last several chapters.

This priestly encouragement that *spurs one another on to love and good deeds* is not only through teaching, but also through prayer and worship. And again, this could come from any believer, not just a worship leader or Bible teacher or prayer coordinator.

About the time I started doing children's ministry, I injured my wrists shovelling snow, and had to wear them both in braces for more than a year. But a little eight-year-old African girl would come up to me every week and ask about my wrists and tell me she was praying for me. Sometimes she even prayed for me right there. I often had tears in my eyes as this faithful little prayer warrior put her hands on my wrists to ask God's healing for me. (They are recovered now—her prayers were answered!)

Neither is singing together just an activity that is done for my aesthetic enjoyment or my private communion with God. Paul describes the rest that can come through corporate worship in Colossians 3:15-16: **Let the peace of Christ rule** *in your hearts... And be thankful. Let the message of Christ dwell among you richly as you teach and admonish one another with all wisdom through psalms, hymns, and songs from the Spirit,* **singing to God with gratitude in your hearts.**

A Communal Catalyst for Encouragement

Whether or not Sunday is observed as an all-day Sabbath by all the people in a particular gathering, that part of the day set aside by the community to be together can become an important communal container for rest, and a valuable Sabbath-time in the week. Even if the nurse must report back that day to the hospital, or the student to studying for tomorrow's exam, maintaining the *habit of meeting together* gives a platform for encouragement that can extend into the week, through calls and emails and meeting over coffee to share hopes and prayers.

We have already briefly noted that the writer to Hebrews, in his great exposition of rest in Hebrews 3 & 4, mentioned this kind of mutual encouragement that we have been considering as an antidote to the hardness of heart that resists rest: *But encourage one another daily, as long as it is called Today, so that none of you may be hardened by sin's deceitfulness* (3:13). The weekly face-to-face of this communal gathering is just the catalyst that is needed in order for this daily encouragement to be possible.

Reflections:

- What keeps you from *meeting together* on a Sunday most often? How would you evaluate your reasons for not attending? What would it take for you to make a regular weekly commitment to your community?
- For you, how much of "going to church" is about duty? Image? Your own personal fulfilment, or your family's? What would look different if it were more about connecting with others and encouraging one another?
- How could you and the others that you have gotten to know in your community become more like priests to one another, bringing each other before God through teaching, prayer and worship? How could you continue this through the week in practical, do-able ways?

Rest definition #16:
Rest = encouragement given and received

17 Daily Disciplines of Rest

*Therefore, holy brothers and sisters, who share in the heavenly calling, **fix your thoughts on Jesus**, whom we acknowledge as our apostle and high priest.* (Hebrews 3:1)

My grandfather always said, "What'll hold a lot'll hold a little." That may be true, but I find I like to match the size of the container to what it is supposed to contain! And as a result, my kitchen cupboards are full of plastic lidded boxes—some large enough to freeze a whole pot of soup, others just big enough to take along dressing for a packed salad lunch, and every size in between.

In the same way, the containers for our rest do not have to come in just one size. A Sabbath day is just the start and focal point for rest that should overflow into other times of our busy week. Tucked in between the work that we are called by God to do, we can create little portable pockets of Sabbath rest in each day that reconnect us to God and his completed works.

Daily Realignment with God's Will & Works

The recipients of Hebrews would have been totally familiar with this concept. It was the habit of godly Jews in the first century to stop to pray three times a day, either on their own or in the synagogue or temple. The outline for this daily prayer was the *Amidah,* or the "Eighteen Benedictions." Each benediction was a prayer heading, so that the person would pray, "Blessed are You, shield of Abraham," and then go on to praise God for his faithfulness to Israel throughout history, and so on through the list. But the format was flexible; if you were in a hurry, you could pray just the outline, rather than elaborating on all of the benedictions.

It was the custom of first-century rabbis to teach their followers a community prayer based on the *Amidah* that could be used as a digest of its main ideas, and also serve as a prayer outline. And that was what Jesus was doing when he said to his disciples: *"This, then, is how you should pray: Our Father in Heaven, hallowed be Your name. Your kingdom come. Your will be done on earth as it is in heaven. Give us today our daily bread. And forgive us our debts, as we also have forgiven our debtors. And lead us not into temptation, but deliver us from the evil one. For yours is the kingdom and the power and the glory forever, Amen."* (Matthew 6:9-13).

As a result, it was common practice for members of the early church to pray the Lord's Prayer three times a day, either alone or together, following the Jewish rhythm. It would not simply have been recited verbatim each time, but also used as an outline of the important topics of prayer:

- Aligning oneself with the Father's glory, kingdom, and will;
- Asking in trust for provision, forgiveness, guidance and deliverance;
- Acknowledging gratefully his eternal power to do all he has purposed.

Think back on what we saw was our basis for rest: the completed work of God in creation and provision, redemption and renewal. Now look closely at what this prayer is saying. It is a daily affirmation of faith in a sovereign God whose purposes are being accomplished in the cosmos, and who is also intensely interested in caring for each of his creatures. What better way to get back to rest than to pray such a prayer on a regular basis?

Modern Rhythms of Daily Rest

Some in our day have continued this rhythm of three-times-a-day prayer, taking a small amount of time to stop and reconnect with their Creator each morning, noon, and evening. In traditional circles, this is called "Praying the Office," and there are many books and online resources that have prayers and Scripture readings that can be used each day to follow this rhythm.

Another common daily discipline is known as the "Quiet Time" or "devotions"—a morning or evening time spent in Bible reading and prayer. Sometimes people will use a Bible reading plan so that they can read through all of it in a year; other times they might concentrate on one book or section. There also exist many daily devotional books that take short sections of Scripture and give a small practical commentary so a person may apply the text to their lives.

One of the dangers of observing a weekly Sabbath day is that we create a false dichotomy of "God's day" and "my days," of sacred vs. secular. But as we make space for Sabbath on the other days, we can blur artificial lines that we have drawn, and view all time as sacred.

Creating Portable Pockets of Rest

Unlike the Sabbath, these containers are not prescribed for us in Scripture. We may choose a daily pattern that fits our schedule and personality, and that may change over time.

The first task in creating these pockets of rest is finding the open spaces in your day. No matter how busy you are, you will find that at some point there are at least twenty free minutes when you can stop your brain's frenetic activity and focus on God. Maybe it is while you are on the treadmill at the gym. Maybe it is during a lunch break at your desk. Maybe it is right after your alarm goes off—if you set it early enough—and while you are drinking your first cup of coffee.

The second task is becoming aware your own alertness patterns and learning styles, and tailoring your disciplines to these. Pick a time to pray when you are most likely to be physically rested and awake, rather than a time when lack of concentration or sleepiness will cause frustration. And if you are an aural learner who finds reading difficult, try listening to an audio Bible and podcasts rather than struggling through devotional books. You can also combine disciplines with other activities, like listening to Scripture and praying while driving to work, or while running. (This can be especially helpful for kinaesthetic learners who process best while in motion, or for aural learners who can hear themselves pray right out loud in their car!)

It embarrasses me to discuss these disciplines with you as though I were good at them. While I am acquainted with people who revel in a rigorous self-imposed regimen, I think I am one of the least naturally-disciplined people I know! The only hope I have of doing this regularly is by following practices that I enjoy at a time that is convenient.

It is like a diet—if you eat food you hate, you won't stick to it. But if you eat stuff you love, it becomes easier. You may feel some initial resistance as you approach the time you have set—this is normal, as our deep-rooted self-reliance fights back—but if you push through this, joy awaits you on the other side as you reaffirm your rest in Jesus. It is worth *making the effort to enter his rest.*

And once again, beware confusing the containers with the contents! Many years ago when I was in Bible college, a Christian song came out called, "I Miss My Time With You." It depicted a sad-eyed Jesus sitting forlornly on the sofa while the singer is off doing a million other things instead of having a "quiet time." The song was made, I am sure, with good intentions—but for me, this was just one more impetus to guilt in the years that followed. I became so focused on whether or not I "missed my time" with Jesus and caused him to be disappointed or angry, that I really forgot that the point was to rest in him. I forgot to enjoy the times I did have, because I was so focused on my own guilt and failure—my personal performance.

If the daily disciplines you already practice have become stale or guilt-producing—or a cause for self-congratulation—then you might consider changing their form. Do something different. Don't give up on *making the effort to enter rest*, but change the container so that the contents will stay fresher.

The point of creating these daily containers is to *fix our eyes on Jesus, the pioneer and perfecter of our faith* (Hebrews 12:2). As he taught us in the Lord's Prayer, we must each day realign ourselves with his will and kingdom, and ask him in trust for our daily needs as well as forgiveness, guidance and protection. It is easy during the course of each day to become entangled again with our own anxieties, to become bogged down in our responsibilities, thinking everything is up to us. Without restful reminders each day, we easily become self-reliant, and our self-effort leads to exhaustion. It is only by *fixing our eyes on Jesus* daily that we will be able to *run with perseverance the race marked out for us* (Hebrews 12:1).

Reflections:

- What are your best "pockets" of time in which you could create daily disciplines that help you to rest in Jesus? When are you most awake and alert? When are you least likely to be interrupted? Most likely to be able to focus?
- What would you like to do in this time?
  - Do you prefer to pray spontaneously? With a plan? With written prayers? A combination?
  - How do you like to interact with the Bible? With a reading plan? A study Bible? A devotional book? Do you remember better if you listen, or read?
  - Do you like to write to process your thoughts? What if you kept a journal or a notebook—noting down things for which you are thankful, insights from Scripture, prayer request and answers, and so on? What about a sketchbook in which you could draw? How would making a record of your thoughts enhance your efforts to rest?
- Have you even gotten confused between the container and the contents when it comes to daily disciplines? How? What could you do to keep your focus on Jesus rather than on your own performance?
- Pray through the Lord's Prayer, using each petition as a starting point for aligning yourself with the Father and expressing your trust for his provision and renewal. How could this be a model for daily rest for you?

Rest definition #17:
Rest = regular realignment with God's will & works

18 XL Containers: Holidays & Leisure

Celebrate the Festival of Tabernacles for seven days after you have gathered the produce of your threshing floor and your winepress. Be joyful at your festival—you, your sons and daughters, your male and female servants, and the Levites, the foreigners, the fatherless and the widows who live in your towns. **For seven days celebrate the festival to the Lord your God** *at the place the Lord will choose. For the Lord your God will bless you in all your harvest and in all the work of your hands, and* **your joy will be complete.** (Deuteronomy 16:13-15)

"Where are you going on holiday?" This question becomes a popular topic of conversation as the summer draws nearer. We share enthusiastically about going to the beach, camping in the forest, hiking in the mountains, seeing Grandma and the cousins. We look forward every year to a break in our schedule when we can put aside our work's demands and spend an extended time resting.

The Holidays of Israel

If you asked an Israelite child this question in Jesus' time, they would know exactly where they were going to spend their holidays—Jerusalem. Every year, their fathers were required to go up to the Temple for the three major holidays, just as Moses had decreed: *Three times a year all your men must appear before the Lord your God at the place he will choose: at the Festival of Unleavened Bread [Passover], the Festival of Weeks [Pentecost] and the Festival of Tabernacles* (Deuteronomy 16:16). And sometimes, the whole family would get to accompany Dad.

These three Jewish festivals were extended times in which each person was to remember God's works of Provision and Redemption, responding with gratitude and generosity in a spirit of joy and celebration. In the Passover feast, the people commemorated their redemption during the Exodus from the Angel of Death, who "passed over" the houses of Israelites sprinkled with the blood of an innocent lamb rather than killing the firstborn inside, as well as their deliverance from the Egyptians. The Feasts of Weeks and Tabernacles were both harvest feasts, times to thank God for his abundant provision for his people; the second of also featured a week spent in temporary shelters to remind them of how God cared for his people during the Exodus, while wandering in the wilderness. (You can read more about these in Leviticus 23.)

What fun! The whole family would get to travel to Jerusalem with friends and cousins, in a crowd of pilgrims from their town. This is how Jesus and his parents got separated from each other travelling back from the Passover—and why it took his parents a whole day to miss him—in the story recorded in Luke 2:41-50. They assumed he was off having a great time with his buddies!

And there were feasts on these holidays as well, with singing and dancing, as the family ate their part of the thank offerings given in gratitude to God. Not to mention that at the Feast of Tabernacles, everyone got to camp out in little huts made of palm leaves! I would imagine that these trips were the highlights of every Jewish kid's year, just like our kids look forward to our annual vacation.

But perhaps not quite like our vacations. For on our holidays, we often forget that the original meaning of the word was "holy days"— days of rejoicing and resting before God.

Our English word comes from the Middle Ages, when a day off that was not a Sunday was arranged around a feast day in the Church calendar. Some of these—such as Easter and Pentecost—were in turn echoes of the ancient holidays of the Israelites. An important part of the holiday, then, would be given over to religious observances intended to mark the fact that it was actually a "holy day," and not just a day off.

Days Set Apart for Me, Myself, and I

In the agrarian societies of ancient Israel and medieval Europe, these religious festivals were the only kind of days off that people had, apart from the weekly Sabbath. The hours, days, and weeks of personal leisure that we take as our right are a much more modern invention. It was not until the late 1800s or early 1900s that the working man won the right to "Eight Hours for Work, Eight Hours for Sleep, Eight Hours for What I Will." And vacations, which started out in the 19th century as either physical "cures" taken at a health resort, or spiritual retreats at Christian conventions, evolved into a yearly time to indulge in sights and sports in pleasure palaces near and far.

The two-day weekend is an even more recent innovation, dating from the 1920s in America. As people started taking half-days on

Saturday, and later the whole day off, it was found that people spent more money on leisure pursuits like going to movies and sports, and had more time to frequent local resorts in their fast cars. The Era of Leisure for All had arrived. And so the focus for days of rest changed from relaxation and contemplation into capitalistic opportunities for dollar-producing activities.

Of course, for many in Europe and America, Sunday was still a day of worship, the "Lord's Day," with many businesses closed and certain activities curtailed. But now we had Saturday as well, a day not for God, but for me—a whole day for "what I will." It doesn't take much to begin to think of the whole weekend as "my time"— and woe betide any one who suggests otherwise.

This emphasis on leisure has continued to grow, so that now many people (particularly in Europe) would say that they work so that they can go on vacation. Work is primarily to earn the money that fuels my leisure pursuits, whether that is during my long lunch, after my 35-hour week, or on my month-long holiday in a sunny and gorgeous location. We have become leisure junkies.

But do we feel any better? Any more rested? Are we ready and raring to go back to work Monday morning or after the package holiday, or just depressed that it is so long till the next break? Are the contents we put in these multiple and large containers for rest filling us up, or making us feel emptier? Does our recreation actually result in re-creation of our souls?

Recapturing the Holiness of Holidays

We are really blessed in our society to have so much discretionary time. We are not forced to work twelve hours for six days a week, doing just one job. We have time to be with our families and friends and to keep in contact with those far away. We have time to pursue hobbies. We have time to travel to interesting places. We have time apart from our regular paid work to do the housework, the laundry, the shopping, the gardening, and still have time left over for other recreation. We have time to invest in projects and causes that we find compelling, in people that need a listening ear or a helping hand.

To recapture the holiness of these holidays, we first need to recognize that leisure time is a blessing from God, richness given from his hand, just as material wealth is. It is fairly commonly recognized by Christians that we are merely stewards or managers of the money that God has entrusted to us, and that we are to use it wisely—as in Psalm 50, where God tells us that *"the world is mine, and all that is in it."*

Isn't this just as true of time, which he created along with the universe? And isn't the time we have been given supposed to be used wisely and reverently, as time belonging to someone else and not to us? Including the time we think of as "my time"?

Sometimes God gives you more leisure to spend on work that he calls you to do—paid or not. That may be an investment in your own family, like growing a family vegetable garden or taking care of your aging mother; or in another's wellbeing, like using your vacation to put up a house for Habitat for Humanity. It may be pursuing an artistic project that he is inspiring you to do, demonstrating his glory through your creativity. It may be a ministry that he has given you.

And sometimes he gives you extra time just to appreciate and enjoy him more—to slow you down when you have been moving too fast. This could be by your own deliberate choice, as when you take a sabbatical or a vacation with family. You may even decide to spend a weekend or holiday intensely focused on your spiritual well-being, by spending time at a Christian conference or retreat, or spending time in quiet contemplation at a monastery or in solitude. But occasionally this happens in a dramatic and unexpected way that God surprises you with, as when surgery forces you to take time for recovery, or when your work status is changed.

A friend of mine lost her full-time job a year or so ago and could only find a part-time job to replace it. This was at first a worry, because she was not making the same amount of money as usual to supplement her husband's pay. But gradually she came to see it as a blessing, as the slower pace allowed her to invest more time in reading and reflection, in investment in relationships. God had given her not just leisure, but real rest, as she recognized him as the source of provision, and invested time in spiritual and relational priorities.

And what about the real "holy days"—holidays that bear a religious significance, such as Christmas and Easter and Pentecost? Like the Israelites of old, perhaps we need to recapture the sense of sacredness in them. It is all too easy to be caught up in the consumerism and greed of our times, and forget, as Deuteronomy text at the beginning of this chapter says, to *celebrate the festival to the Lord your God,* and that in this *your joy will be complete.*

As we recognize all of our time—including the time formerly thought of as "my time"—as God's, and are grateful to him for it, then we will not begrudge him the time that we invest as Sabbath, times dedicated to him, but recognize that these as the starting point for our most profound rest. And we will look for his calling as to how to invest for him the rest of these riches, the incredible amount of leisure time he has given us—whether in work, in ministry to others, or in enjoying in God's presence his world and his gifts to us.

This is part of the minute-by-minute *Sabbath rest* we have been looking at, that Hebrews 4 calls us into—resting in faith in the Creator who has provided for us, the Redeemer who is renewing us. The Jewish festivals focused on gratitude to God for his provision and redemption. So what would it take for you to come back from your next vacation grateful, instead of grumpy?

Reflections:
- Would you see yourself as more focused on work or leisure in your life? What do you think are the dangers of being too focused on work? What are the dangers of seeing work as simply a way to finance our leisure pursuits?
- Does your leisure time usually feel restful to you or not? If not, what is it that you think robs you of that rest?
- For some of us, it is a stretch to think of *some* of our time as belonging to God (one day in seven). What difference does it make to perceive *all* our time as belonging to God? What do you think it means to be a **manager** of the time we have rather than the **possessor** of it?
- When have you made a deliberate choice to slow down and spend time appreciating God and all that he has given you for an extended period? Have you ever seen God slow you down in an unexpected way?
- How could you celebrate actual "holy days" (such as Easter, Christmas, and Pentecost) so that you could recapture their original meaning?
- What **would** it take for you to come back from your next vacation grateful, instead of grumpy?

Rest definition #18
Rest ≠ "Me Time"

part four:
filling the containers
with real rest

19 Counterfeit Contents

"If you keep your feet from breaking the Sabbath
  and from doing as you please on my holy day,
if you call the Sabbath a delight
  and the Lord's holy day honourable,
and if you honour it by not going your own way
  and not doing as you please or speaking idle words,
then you will find your joy in the Lord,
  and I will cause you to ride in triumph on the heights of the land
  and to feast on the inheritance of your father Jacob."
    (Isaiah 58:13-14)

You've seen them: the magazine articles that urge you to *Find Time for 'Me Time'* and *Put Yourself on the Priority List*. It's clear why these articles exist—especially in America, where overwork is a kind of epidemic, with many people working more than 50 hours a week, and one in seven taking no vacation. No wonder these enticements to (badly needed) rest are so appealing.

They certainly are to me. But one of the basic problems I face when I **do** take time off is that it becomes—as the ads indicate—all about me. I rely on myself to suck all the rest out of the day, to soothe myself and make myself feel good. I want to make the decision of what contents I put into my leisure container, with no one else to tell me what to do. Having worked hard, I want to play hard, to fill my time off with the pleasure that I deserve.

But "Me Time" and "Sabbath" are not exactly the same thing...

Lovers of Pleasure

We live in a culture of narcissism, where we feel entitled to the best that life has to offer and look for everything we can to serve ourselves. We hear the message over and over again: "Take a break—You deserve it!" We are told to pamper ourselves, to look after Number One. We feel like any time off work is our right, our possession to be used primarily for our own gratification.

Perversely, people may overwork just to achieve the level of comfort and pleasure that they want to experience in their down time—to make enough money to afford the pool and jaccuzzi, the exotic vacation, and the comfortable retirement. It is reminiscent of the Rich Fool in Jesus' parable we looked at earlier in Luke 16:16-21: always building bigger barns to store up what is saved, looking forward to taking life easy on the excess—only to find that death comes too soon.

Even for those of us that try to observe Sabbath times, times dedicated to God, it is easy for us to delineate between "God's time" and "my time." Then we fill the container of Sabbath times with the things we think we *should* be doing (like going to church or "having a quiet time") and fill up the rest of our off-work time with what *we* want to do, with a focus on our own pleasure. "God's time" can easily become a mere form, something we do to keep him happy and off our back, while we rely for our real refreshment on the rest we create for ourselves.

In Jesus' Parable of the Sower, we can see what happens to our rest when we are like this: *The seed that fell among thorns stands for those who hear, but as they go on their way they are choked by life's worries, riches and pleasures, and they do not mature* (Luke 8:14).

2 Timothy 3:2-5 describes the kind of people we are in danger of becoming, as we live in these *last days*: "*People will be lovers of themselves, lovers of money... **lovers of pleasure rather than lovers of God**—having a form of godliness but denying its power.*"

It is a curious thing, but when we are simply *lovers of pleasure*, pleasure begins to lose its luster. As the writer of Ecclesiastes reported, "*I denied myself nothing my eyes desired; I refused my heart no pleasure... Yet when I surveyed all that my hands had done and what I had toiled to achieve, **everything was meaningless**, a chasing after the wind; nothing was gained under the sun*" (Ecclesiastes 2:10-11, edited).

No doubt for Phoebe in our prologue, pizza, wine and TV at first felt like a kind of pleasurable reward for all of the hard work she had done that day. But repeated day after day, it loses its gratification. And Bill the paper salesman is trying to recreate the old sense of excitement he used to find in football by watching games at work—but it eludes him.

The truth is: creature comforts are not sufficient for real rest. When the container of our discretionary time is filled up with a focus on personal pleasure, it turns out to be a counterfeit of the contents that would cause us to truly rest.

Enjoying Ourselves in God's Presence

But the paradox is that when we are *lovers of God*, the pleasures that he grants to us, and the time that he allows us to enjoy them, take on an extra brightness.

God made us as people who experience pleasure, and he wants us to enjoy all that he has given to us. But most of all, he wants us to enjoy it **with** him, and in thankfulness to him for his provision. Romans 14:23 tells us that *everything that does not come from faith is sin*; but the opposite is also true. Every enjoyable activity that is done in faith, savoured in the presence and blessing of God, is a good work done before him. I can take a bubble bath, play a squash game, or enjoy a café meal in the sun under his loving eye, with enjoyment enhanced by gratitude for the gift I have been given, rather than a sense of entitlement—or guilt. This is part of the spiritual rest Hebrews 4 has taught us.

But I can also spend time on others—my children, my parents, my friends—without grudging their cutting into "my time." I can do the Saturday chores without resentment, thankful that God has given me time apart from my paid work to do this work also, and grateful that there is still a day to rest on the weekend. I can choose to invest my leisure in service to others—whether a free afternoon at an orphanage or a mission trip on my vacation.

We are fortunate in our era to have so much discretionary time, time in which we can not only physically rest, but also further God's kingdom purposes. We can choose to fill these containers with things that will give us real rest, based on our recognition of God's providence and redemption in our lives. Over the next few chapters, we want to look at **what really restful things we can put in these containers of free time,** and especially in the times we have designated as devoted to God—Sabbath times.

Enjoying God on the Sabbath

Have a look again at the text from Isaiah at the beginning of the chapter. At first glance, it may seem quite restrictive to us. And indeed, many have interpreted these verses as prohibiting the practice of anything that is pleasurable on the Sabbath day. My own background comes from the old Scots Presbyterians, who in days gone by would eat cold oatmeal all day and spend Sunday afternoon sitting on straight-backed chairs studying their catechism between the morning and evening church services. While my upbringing was not nearly this prohibitive, we were forbidden to watch TV or do any sort of sport on Sunday. This led to some rather fine distinctions, as it was deemed okay to run through the sprinklers on a hot day (this *was* in warm Western Australia, after all) but not to jump in a pool.

However, I believe that what God is saying through Isaiah in this text is not that we should do nothing fun or pleasurable on the Sabbath. Rather, we should take our pleasure in Him first, instead than thinking of this non-work time as just another hunk of "my time." Jesus told us that *"the Sabbath was made for man"*—but it was made so that people could have the chance to reconnect with the One who made both it and them. When that purpose is ignored, the Sabbath loses its joy-making value.

In Jewish culture, the Sabbath is greeted with joy, like a bride, as the candles are lit at sundown. Those in mourning are forbidden to display public signs of it for the day. It is treated as a feast rather than a fast, with three festive meals being eaten. Each of these meals is preceded by a blessing spoken over the bread, the braided *challah*, symbolic of the double portion of manna that God caused to fall on the day before Sabbath in the wilderness. Wine is also blessed and drunk. Family comes together. Songs are sung. And one of the encouraged activities for the day is that couples engage in marital relations with one other (in contrast with my Presbyterian forbears)! There is much we could learn from this approach...

Is Sabbath a fast or a feast? An interesting combination of the two. For as we fast from simply *doing as we please*, and focus on the One who is the Source of our joy, we will find that Sabbath is a feast. We will, as Isaiah tells us, *find our joy in the Lord.* And we will find that the pleasures we enjoy as *lovers of God* take on an extra brightness, not only in Sabbath times, but in other times as well.

Reflections:

- Read Amos 6:1-7. How does leisure lead to complacency in our own lives? What kind of catastrophe could this lead to for us, as it did for the leisured classes of Amos' day?
- What do you think it looks like to be a *lover of pleasure rather than a lover of God* in your attitude toward leisure time? Are you afraid of God taking your pleasures away? What difference would it make to see the pleasures that you enjoy as God's gift? How does that increase your love for the Giver?
- How do you think that enjoying the activities that you love **along with** God, rather than relying on the pleasures alone for comfort, might enhance your experience of them?

One hymn writer wrote about this experience this way:

> Heaven above is softer blue
> Earth around is sweeter green
> Something lives in every hue
> Christless eyes have never seen
> Birds with gladder songs o'erflow
> Flowers with deeper beauties shine
> Since I know, as now I know
> I am His, and He is mine.

Rest definition #19:
Rest = finding pleasure in loving God

20 Refrain from Work

There are six days when you may work, but the seventh day is a day of sabbath rest, a day of sacred assembly. **You are not to do any work**; *wherever you live, it is a sabbath to the Lord.* (Leviticus 23:3)

My grandmother's neighbor—an Orthodox Jewish rabbi—came to her door one Saturday needing her help. Certainly, she replied, and followed him to his apartment. They climbed the stairs and went into the kitchen, where he asked her to open his refrigerator. At first she did not see anything amiss, for the fridge was definitely working.

But then he pointed to the corner near the door of the fridge, and she noticed that a piece of duct tape over the light switch had come loose, so that instead of staying on permanently, it lit up whenever the door was opened. This was a problem for the rabbi, whose laws prevented him from "lighting a fire" on the Sabbath—and now he was doing it inadvertently by opening his fridge! My grandmother replaced the duct tape so that everything was kosher again, and the rabbi returned to his rest.

Sabbath Laws in the Old Testament

If you look up the Old Testament injunctions regarding the Sabbath, it is surprising to find that very few of them have to do with the kinds of things we would expect for a holy day. There are a couple of extra sacrifices prescribed for the priests, and the showbread is changed in the Temple. The text above is the only one that mentions it as *a day of sacred assembly.* But every Sabbath command emphatically mentions that *you are not to do any work.* This, more than anything else, even what we might consider religious behavior, is the main distinctive of the Sabbath; it is what "sets apart" the day to God.

This becomes less surprising when you realize that the word "Sabbath" is itself an intensification of the Hebrew word for "repose," and related to the words for "cessation" and "to sit." It indicates not merely doing nothing, but **actively** resting—as can be seen in its relation to another modern Hebrew word, *shevita*, which means "a labour strike." Resting in the Sabbath sense was meant to be a deliberate act, a sit-down strike from all the work done in the rest of the week!

As we noted before, this deliberate act of refraining from work was serious and all-encompassing in the Old Testament:

- It was **for everyone** in the community, even the working animals: *Six days do your work, but on the seventh day do not work, so that **your ox** and **your donkey** may rest, and so that **the slave** born in your household and **the foreigner** living among you may be refreshed* (Exodus 23:12).
- It was even **for times when the workload was heavy:** *Six days you shall labor, but on the seventh day you shall rest; **even during the plowing season and harvest you must rest.*** (Exodus 34:21)
- The **punishment for working on the Sabbath was severe:** *For six days work is to be done, but the seventh day is a day of sabbath rest, holy to the Lord. **Whoever does any work on the Sabbath day is to be put to death.*** (Exodus 31:15)

This is not to say that this commandment was universally followed. The Israelites often saw the Sabbath as a convenient day for doing as they pleased, including the opportunity to carry on business. Jeremiah saw fit to warn the people of Jerusalem that the Lord would judge their city for the repeated ignoring of this command not to work by themselves and their ancestors: *"But if you do not obey me to keep the Sabbath day holy by not carrying any load as you come through the gates of Jerusalem on the Sabbath day, then I will kindle an unquenchable fire in the gates of Jerusalem that will consume her fortresses"* (look up Jeremiah 17:21-27). The destruction of Jerusalem not long after this indicates that Jeremiah's warning went unheeded.

A Return to Sabbath-Keeping

On their return to Judea, many Jewish people wanted to be careful not to make the same mistakes as their ancestors had. The rabbis in the inter-testamental period became concerned about keeping these laws more conscientiously than their forefathers, and developed a set of detailed laws defining prohibited activities for Sabbath. This eventually entailed 39 categories of activity, ranging from such things as "plowing earth" and "shearing wool" to "making two loops" and "erasing two or more letters." Within these categories many more activities were defined as prohibited, which is why in Mark 2 the disciples were charged with the forbidden activity of "reaping" for plucking a few heads of grain. And also why my grandmother's neighbor needed her help with his light switch in order not to be a Sabbath-breaker.

The pendulum had swung the other way. Now instead of being Sabbath-breakers, observant Jews such as the Pharisees had become meticulous about Sabbath minutiae. Instead of their minds being occupied with work on the Sabbath, their minds easily became occupied with the intricate business of **avoiding** working, with decisions about the morality of each little action. (Not to mention passing judgment on the Sabbath actions of those around them...)

Deliberately Resting from Our Work

How do we learn from the experience of Israel now, in our day, under a New Covenant? Clearly, one thing that we can do to fill our Sabbath containers with real rest is to abstain from work. More than that, we can do it on a regular basis, not just when there is little to do, or when we are all finished with a task or project. The fact that this rest is based in creation, not just Mosaic law, and is part of the Ten Commandments (the rest of which we accept as morally normative today), suggests that this is something that could be to our benefit as well as theirs.

Over and over we must remind ourselves—**why** is it so important not to work? The reason is just as we saw in Hebrews 4:10: *Anyone who enters God's rest also rests from their works, just as God did from his.* The deliberate act of stopping work is a practical and prophetic demonstration of this spiritual reality. It is a constructive confession that it is not "all up to me." God is ultimately the one who will provide and renew, and even though he involves me in these works, for this one day I can set them aside and leave all of it up to him in a very tangible way.

Deliberate and active rest takes effort. It means we might have to make preparation to rest, like finishing up a project on Saturday we would usually drag out for a whole weekend. It might mean laying aside something we are working on and telling ourselves we will not pay attention to it for a set time. It might mean working harder one day so the next can be cleared.

I experienced this as a child in an observant Sabbatarian household. Saturday mornings were for me not a time to watch cartoons, but to start my homework so I would be sure to get it done before Sunday came, when homework was not allowed. As a naturally distracted and procrastinating kid, I quite often stayed at my desk far longer than was necessary for the work to get done. But then, on Sunday, it was worth it. I never had to feel guilty or anxious about homework. I could invite a friend home for lunch after church. I could read a book without interruption. I could munch popcorn and play games with my family on Sunday night.

A friend whose grown daughter celebrates a Jewish-style Sabbath as a Christian told me that when visiting her, they all were requested to refrain from even talking about their work, in keeping with Isaiah 58's injunction against *"speaking idle words"* on that day. This my friend at first found difficult, as it turns out that North Americans spend a lot of their conversation on this topic! But gradually, she said, it led to conversations that never would have happened otherwise—refreshing exchanges that lifted life out of the normal.

This is a totally different approach than working till you drop, and then resting when you can't do any more. It involves planning and determination. It involves deliberately stopping even when (and maybe especially when) pressures are high. But the rewards of resting from work one day in seven can be worth it.

Different Convictions, Different Practices

How we put this concept into practice will differ according to our convictions of what God is calling us to. For some of us, even setting aside one afternoon a week when we don't check our email or work on something to do with our business is a stretch, requiring a great deal of planning and effort. Others may feel called to observe a whole day. Still others may choose to take a more rigorous approach, even following the Jewish example in an attempt to experience a deeper closeness with Jesus. In Romans 14:5-6, Paul says, *"One person considers one day more sacred than another; another considers every day alike. **Each of them should be fully convinced in their own mind.** Whoever regards one day as special does so to the Lord."*

The important thing is that these choices are made out of freedom and joy, and the conviction that one is doing what God is calling them to do. They should not be made because someone else told you that this is how it must be done. Rather, you must dialogue with God yourself about how he would have you obey this principle of resting regularly from your work. How would he have **you** physically and prophetically demonstrate the words of the writer of Hebrews: *There remains, then, a Sabbath-rest for the people of God;* ***for anyone who enters God's rest also rests from their works,*** *just as God did from his* (4:9-10)?

Paul goes on to say in Romans 14, "*So then, each of us will give an account of ourselves to God. Therefore let us stop passing judgment on one another. Instead, make up your mind not to put any stumbling block or obstacle in the way of a brother or sister...* **Let us therefore make every effort to do what leads to peace *and* to mutual edification...** *So whatever you believe about these things keep between yourself and God*" (v. 12-13, 19, 22).

Thus the even **more** important thing than how we celebrate Sabbath is that we do not judge others for how they choose to celebrate time with God, as the Pharisees did. Rather, we should encourage one another to "get some rest," and be people whose lives are not all about our own work, but about God's.

Reflections:

- Why do you think God was so insistent on this particular rule for the Sabbath in the Old Testament? What was he trying to facilitate for his people? Why did it matter whether they worked or not?
- What would deliberately resting from your work look like for you? What would you have to stop doing? What kinds of preparation would you have to make in order to do this? What would you have to turn off? What would you have to lay aside and just not worry about?
- Do you currently observe any kind of Sabbath during which you abstain from work? If so, what are your reasons for observing it as you do? If not, is there a time you could dedicate to God by deliberately refraining from work? When?
- Pray about how God might have you demonstrate your spiritual rest in him by physically resting from your work on a weekly basis.

Rest definition #20:
Rest = regularly stopping your normal work

21 Rest Physically

In peace I will lie down and sleep, for you alone, Lord, make me dwell in safety. (Psalm 4:8)

God could have made us as perpetual motion machines. We could have been fashioned as people who just kept on working, kept on going, kept on functioning as long as we had the correct fuel. But he didn't. He made us to sleep. He provided a container (called night) that we must fill with physical rest every sundown if we want to stay alive and sane.

We take it for granted that we spend almost a third of our lives with all of our senses basically shut down, vulnerable and defenceless. We cannot accomplish anything practical during this time. We cannot make money, or organize events, or clean stuff, or build things. We can only rest.

Which is not to say that there is not a lot going on while we sleep. It is while we sleep that growth takes place and tissue damage is repaired. Hormones that regulate appetite and alertness are released. Our dreams also consolidate our memory, and help us begin unconsciously to work on and solve problems, both emotional and intellectual, that we are facing in our lives. God made sleep to physically refuel and replenish us for all that we do while awake. Sleep is truly a gift that we too often take for granted.

The Spiritual Implications of Sleep

But sleep also has theological connotations, and whether we sleep in peace may be impacted by what we believe. In sleep we are vulnerable. We cannot see the burglar breaking into the house, and if we are deeply asleep, we may not hear him either. We cannot tell if there is a fire starting in the wiring. We must either stay awake and vigilant all night, or take turns keeping watch like men at war—or we have to trust that our security is in God's hands, and sleep *in peace*, as in Psalm 4:8 (quoted at the beginning of this chapter).

Now this does not mean that we don't take sensible precautions, and lock the front door against burglars at night. Nor does it mean that a fire **won't** ever start in the wiring. These things happen. But they happen under God's sovereign control. So we say with the Psalmist: *You alone, Lord, make me dwell in safety,* as we pray for his protection, and rest secure that we are in his hands. And then we can sleep, vulnerable, but protected in the only meaningful way, by the God who never sleeps:

> He will not let your foot slip—
>> he who watches over you will not slumber;
> indeed, he who watches over Israel
>> will neither slumber nor sleep. (Psalm 121:3-4)

Sleepless Anxiety

One of the most common causes of insomnia is anxiety. We cannot fall asleep, or we wake up with a start in the night, because the crowd of troubles and worries start a noise in our heads that is so deafening as to drive off sleep. We lie staring into the darkness, our thoughts running like a hamster wheel: How can I solve that conflict with my colleague? What if my husband leaves me? What is my child at university doing right now? How am I going to pay off the car? How can I get my father to quit drinking so much? What if my job is the next one axed? Could that pain in my abdomen be something serious, like cancer?

This is where belief in a God whose *work is finished* is crucial. To know he **will** provide for you—even if not in ways you expect, even if you lose your job and your house and all. To know that he **is** in the business of renewal, and that he cares more than you do about your kid in college, or your alcoholic father.

This is also where prayer before sleep can help, dispelling the anxieties of the day, letting them go as you give them over to the One who *neither slumbers nor sleeps.* He is both Eternal Work, ceaselessly labouring on behalf of his creation, and Eternal Rest, always contemplating his finished work from a timeless perspective. And then we can say with the Psalmist:

> I call out to the Lord,
>> and he answers me from his holy mountain.
> I lie down and sleep;
>> I wake again, because the Lord sustains me.
> I will not fear though tens of thousands
>> assail me on every side. (Psalm 3:4-6)

Fall Asleep Counting Your Blessings

A discipline that I have found even better than praying through my anxieties before sleep is suggested in a little song that Bing Crosby used to sing:

> If you're worried and you can't sleep
> Just count your blessings instead of sheep
> And you'll fall asleep counting your blessings...

We do not want to make the same mistakes as the ancient Israelites, forgetting how God has provided for us and delivered us in the past because we are so focused on present troubles. Rather, a night-time habit of meditating on what God has done for you and thanking him for it makes it easier to trust that he is truly *watching over* you in whatever situations you are facing.

And when you start to really count, you will be surprised how the blessings add up. For a while, I always started with thanking God for my pillow—an extremely comfortable one that I take everywhere with me. And that always led to something else I was thankful for, which led to something else again. It's okay to fall asleep in the middle of this kind of prayer, because it is really never finished!

Sleep and Sabbath

When I was in Bible college, I really looked forward to my Sunday afternoon nap! This is a practice that my husband and I have continued to follow since then. It is amazing how easy it is to follow a discipline that you enjoy!

In Jewish culture, as well, the Sabbath is a time to catch up on some extra physical rest by sleeping. Perhaps not all of us want to take a nap, but maybe we would enjoy the opportunity to sleep in a bit and go to the late church service, or get to bed a bit earlier than usual. Of course, this opportunity is facilitated by the last practice we discussed—that of refraining from work.

But even if we don't feel the need for extra sleep, a Sabbath time can be an opportunity for our bodies to rest as well as our souls. It is a time when we may simply sit and reflect, to allow our muscles to relax from their tension as we meditate on God's goodness to us, on the fact that our work is in his hands.

He Grants Sleep To Those He Loves

The year my daughter was born, Michael Card had just come out with a lovely album of lullabies for babies, largely based on Scripture, called "Sleep Sound in Jesus." We played and sang the songs over and over, and it was the first time in my life that I had thought of sleep as a precious gift of God. (Perhaps that was also because, as a new mother, I was getting relatively little of it!) One of his songs had an intriguing title taken from Psalm 127:1-2 (in bold below) that made me pay attention for the first time those verses:

> Unless the Lord builds the house, the builders labour in vain.
> Unless the Lord watches over the city, the guards stand watch in vain.
> In vain you rise early and stay up late, toiling for food to eat
> —for **he grants sleep to those he loves.**

When we look at the basis for peaceful sleep in this psalm, it turns out that it is exactly what we have been considering: God's own work in the world. He is the One who makes our work prosper, when it is based on his own will and work. He is the One who is our true security. Burning the candle at both ends does not guarantee security or prosperity—only exhaustion. We do well to put our work and our wealth in his hands and sleep for the night, trusting that God will multiply our efforts according to his will.

And when we do, we may find when we awaken that our perspective is changed. When we are tired, tasks are more difficult, troubles are greater, temptation is more irresistible. One of our Bible college professors used to say, "Sometimes the most spiritual thing you can do is take a nap." As beings whose physicality and spirituality are inextricably entwined, we do well to heed this advice, and gratefully, trustingly, accept God's gift of sleep that he gives to *those he loves.*

Reflections:

Rest definition #21:
Rest = sleeping sound in Jesus

- Do you regard sleep as a gift from God? Why do you think God made us as creatures who need sleep? What does it teach us or help us remember?
- How have you seen your troubles or temptations multiply when you are not physically rested?
- Do you ever suffer from insomnia because of anxiety? How could giving over that anxiety to God, or counting your blessings, help to alleviate your sleeplessness?
- How could "letting go" of your need to control your safety and productivity produce more restful sleep for you?
- How could you fill a Sabbath time with physical, as well as spiritual, rest?

22 Revere God and Reflect

The fear of the Lord leads to life;
*   then one rests content, untouched by trouble.* (Proverbs 19:23)

When we eat, we feel full, and we gain energy for our activities. When we sleep, we feel refreshed, and we gain alertness for our undertakings. When we exercise, we feel stronger (eventually!), and we gain strength for our endeavours.

And the verse above tells us that when we *fear the Lord,* we will *rest content, untouched by trouble.* This does not mean that trouble will not come—it inevitably will—but that when it does our rest and peace will be so deep as to be undisturbed by it.

But in order to be full, we must give time to meals. In order to be refreshed, we must devote time to sleeping. In order to be fit and strong, we must dedicated time to exercise. In the same way, in order to *rest content,* time also must be committed to cultivating the *fear of the Lord.*

When we looked at Psalm 95, quoted so extensively by the writer to Hebrews, we noted that it called us first to worship God as our Creator who cares for us and our Deliverer who sets us free. And we noted that it was because of the lack of this worship that the first Israelites failed to enter the rest provided for them.

We are encouraged in Scripture to stop our daily work not only so that we can rest physically and mentally, but also so that we can clear our schedules and our minds to be able to see God clearly and appreciate his wonderful works.

Time to Praise God

Psalm 92 is subtitled, *"A psalm, a song for the Sabbath day."* These are the first five verses:

> *It is good to praise the Lord*
> *   and make music to your name, O Most High,*
> *proclaiming your love in the morning*
> *   and your faithfulness at night,*
> *to the music of the ten-stringed lyre*
> *   and the melody of the harp.*

For you make me glad by your deeds, Lord;
  I sing for joy at what your hands have done.
How great are your works, Lord,
  how profound your thoughts!

He then goes on to praise God for his triumph over evil in the world, and for defeating *"my wicked foes"*—all the forces that would oppose God's works in the world. He ends by saying,

The righteous will flourish like a palm tree,
  they will grow like a cedar of Lebanon;
planted in the house of the Lord,
  they will flourish in the courts of our God.
They will still bear fruit in old age,
  they will stay fresh and green,
proclaiming, "The Lord is upright;
  he is my Rock, and there is no wickedness in him."

This last is a metaphorical picture of the perfect rest pictured in Proverbs: a flourishing, fruitful tree, always fresh and green, rooted in the Rock. Look up Psalm 92 for yourself. In it, you will see a pattern for worshipping our way into rest:

- Affirming who God is (here, his attributes of *love* and *faithfulness*)
- Affirming his completed works (*"I sing for joy at what your hands have done"*)
- Gratitude for how God has acted on our behalf (*"fine oils have been poured on me"*)
- Putting our own troubles in perspective through resting in him now and for the future (*"The righteous will flourish like a palm tree…"*)

This is not an isolated pattern, but is seen in many of the psalms. In Psalm 16, for example, the psalmist starts off by affirming what he knows to be true about God and his works, and ends with this statement of trust: *Therefore my heart is glad and my tongue rejoices; my body also will rest secure…*

In Sabbath times—whether a day set aside for worship or a half hour in the morning—this kind of prayer pattern is something that will strengthen us to rest even as we work, to face the struggles and problems of the day. Whether through musical worship like the

Psalmist, or through prayer, we can lift him up along with all his works. As we focus on who God is and praise him for what he has done, the self-reliance that is our bane can be banished.

Time to Gain Wisdom

But how do we know who God is and what he has done? Thank God! He has told us in his Word—revealed it in history, confirmed it in prophecy, outlined it in law, sung it in poetry. This is not just some metaphysical book of high thoughts and lovely philosophy, but the Scripture of which the author of Hebrews said, "*The word of God is alive and active. Sharper than any double-edged sword, it penetrates even to dividing soul and spirit, joints and marrow; it judges the thoughts and attitudes of the heart*" (4:12). Paul described it as "*the Holy Scriptures, **which are able to make you wise** for salvation through faith in Christ Jesus*" (2 Timothy 3:15).

We start to recognize God's voice more and more as we read the letter he has written to us. And then we will understand the voice of the Holy Spirit as he whispers to us, and he in turn will open up more of God's word to make us wise. This is a wisdom that also leads to rest, as Proverbs 3:21-24 tells us:

> *My son, do not let wisdom and understanding out of your sight,*
> *preserve sound judgment and discretion;*
> *they will be life for you,*
> *an ornament to grace your neck.*
> *Then you will go on your way in safety,*
> *and your foot will not stumble.*
> ***When you lie down, you will not be afraid;***
> ***when you lie down, your sleep will be sweet.***

As we dedicate time to God, part of it should be spent in the getting of wisdom. Observant Jews spend part of each of their Sabbaths in the reading, study and discussion of Torah. We can do this too, whether in community with other believers or by ourselves—both experiences are valuable to our hearing God's Word. In community, we see things in Scripture that we might otherwise be blind to, and we have the opportunity to *spur one another on toward love and good deeds* (Hebrews 10:24). But it is also important to have time when God can speak alone into the silence of your own soul as you read what the Holy Spirit has inspired to be written.

And for that, you will need a little quiet…

Time to Be Still

In the middle of a busy time of ministry, Jesus gave an invitation to his disciples: *"Come with me by yourselves to a quiet place and get some rest"* (Mark 6:31). It is an invitation that he also extends to us daily and weekly, and for extended times of quiet retreat. And in that quiet place we can begin to obey the command of Psalm 46:10: **"Be still and know that I am God."**

It is especially tough in our busy lives and busy cities and suburbs to find a place to be still. Buses and trucks rumble by. Babies cry. Our phones ring perpetually, stereos and televisions mask the background noise with constant sound. And more than that, we are often actually uncomfortable with silence and stillness. We are nervous away from our email or social networking sites or mobile phones. We don't know how to cope without a nonstop iPod soundtrack blasting in our ears.

I don't enjoy stillness naturally. As a high-input person, I find deprivation of something to listen to or look at extremely unnerving. Put me in a dark silent room for ten minutes with nothing but a candle and I get the heebie-jeebies. Not only that, but when I attempt to meditate on a simple but profound concept, I find that my concentration wanders nearly immediately and I start wondering about what that black spot on the ceiling is or what I should have for lunch. I have friends who are natural contemplatives, but as much as I admire them, I am not one. So does this mean I am off the hook for *being still?*

No. There are many things that a high-input person like me can do to contemplate creation, to reflect on God and his works, to meditate on Scripture and allow space for the Spirit to speak.

One thing to do to is to fast from technology that will distract or interrupt me for a certain period of time, whether that is a half hour each morning or a whole day or more. A friend of mine in ministry told me about his "Technology-Free Tuesdays," when during the day he would turn off the TV and radio, put away his mobile phone, and even close his computer, writing only by hand. He could not do this on Sunday because of his church responsibilities, but he used these Tuesdays as an opportunity for more stillness and simplicity in his life—for being available to listen to God rather than everyone else for a while.

Another to do is to get out in the wild. One thing I love about meditating on God and his works in nature is that every bit of input I receive simply reinforces my meditation! I can sit still on a log or stone and just open my eyes to contemplate what God has done and to marvel at how "very good" it is.

There are also ways to meditate while still getting input. *Lectio divina* is a method that listens to a Scripture passage read aloud multiple times, as you open yourself up to the Holy Spirit to impress the text on your conscience as he wishes. It is a very different approach than the exegetical one that I usually use for Bible study, a method that is more about heart than head. This method is normally done in community, but with audio Bibles, it is also possible do it alone.

Written prayers and hymns can be very deep sources for reflection and meditation, the words occupying the eyes while the meaning occupies the heart. In the same way, writing out your own prayers causes you to slow down and think about your words and focuses your concentration. I have often found that praying while occupying my hands with some routine task—sewing or washing dishes—helps me to direct my thoughts better. Recently I read of a woman who knits while she prays. The things she makes turn into fluffy, tangible prayer diaries!

The essence of any Sabbath time is time dedicated to God—not just resting physically, not just doing religious things, but also actually being with him. Then we will find this Sabbath rest permeating each day as we trust more and more in our wonderful God. As the writer to the Hebrews says: "*Therefore, since we are receiving a kingdom that cannot be shaken, let us be thankful, and so worship God acceptably with reverence and awe...*" (12:28).

Reflections:

Rest definition #22:
Rest = meditating on God's works and Word

- Look back at the pattern for "worshipping into rest" that we looked at in Psalm 92. Now look at Psalm 16. Do you see a similar pattern here? Can you outline it?
  - o In Psalm 92, the psalmist is already singing at the beginning of the psalm, whereas in Psalm 16, he "*says*" statements about God.   How might these reflect two different starting moods for worship? Why do you think they still end up in the same place?
- How do you spend Sabbath time processing God's Word and letting it shape you? With others? By yourself? (Doing both is ideal!)
- Do you find it easy or hard to be still and meditate on God and his Word to you? Were there any ideas for stillness from this chapter that you would like to try to incorporate into your own practice? Any others you have heard of?

23 Reinforce Relationships

*There are six days when you may work, but the seventh day is a day of sabbath rest, **a day of sacred assembly*** (Leviticus 23:3a)

*Every day they continued to meet together in the temple courts. **They broke bread in their homes and ate together*** *with glad and sincere hearts, praising God and enjoying the favor of all the people.* (Acts 2:46-47)

Sunday lunch at the Kenney's house! What an adventure! You never know exactly who you are going to meet...

Tom and Mabel Kenney are the pastor and his wife at Peninsula Community Chapel in York County, Virginia, where we attended church when we were first married. Every Sunday they host people in their home for lunch. Mabel makes things like lasagne and salad—comfort food that everyone likes. And Tom spots at church whomever is new, and whomever else would mix well with them, and invites them over. The group is always different. The lady who just moved into the neighbourhood. The missionaries on furlough. The disabled guy on his own. The dinner is prepared for us, but the people are potluck.

A Day of Sacred Assembly

The Kenneys are following in a long tradition of Sabbath meals dating from ancient times. We looked in Chapter 16 at the importance of the communal container of common worship for our rest. But the practice of reinforcing relationships, and forging new ones, is an important part of the contents of our Sabbath containers, in addition to our normal church gatherings.

Even today, observant Jews take the Sabbath as an opportunity to get together with family and neighbours, eating festive meals in their homes. It brings to mind the festivals of old, when **everyone** would come together to celebrate and feast: *Be joyful at your festival—you, your sons and daughters, your male and female servants, and the Levites, the foreigners, the fatherless and the widows who live in your towns* (Deuteronomy 16:14). That's quite a list of people!

One of the things they were eating together was the *fellowship offering* described in Leviticus 7:11-18—offered by a worshipper *as an expression of thankfulness* to God. This was the only sacrifice that that was eaten not only by the priests, but also by the giver. The internal organs were burned on the altar, and the shoulder given to the priest as his part. But the rest of the meat was returned to the giver, and had to be eaten that same day. So what did one do with all that meat? Share it with others!

In this way the thankfulness and rejoicing was spread through the whole community, and the recognition of God's provision by one person resulted in provision for their neighbours. It also, no doubt, resulted in some stories and laughter and good times!

The New Testament church continued this practice of *meeting together.* The met not only in the Temple as mentioned in Acts 2 (the text at the beginning of this chapter), but also *broke bread in their homes and ate together with glad and sincere hearts.* They were known for their hospitality. It was not only one of the requirements for leadership in the church (1 Timothy 3:2-3) but even for widows who were to be put on the church's support list (1 Timothy 5:9-10)! Even those who were the poorest of the poor were expected to be part of this ethos.

Resting in Christ is a Team Sport

We are meant to rest in **Christ** alone, but we are not meant to rest in Christ **alone**, if you get my drift. As we already noted, the writer to Hebrews, in helping his weary readers, gives them lots of encouragement not to run their marathon of endurance by themselves:

- But **encourage one another daily,** *as long as it is called "Today," so that none of you may be hardened by sin's deceitfulness* (3:13).
- *And let us consider how we may* **spur one another on toward love and good deeds,** *not giving up meeting together, as some are in the habit of doing, but encouraging one another—and all the more as you see the Day approaching* (10:24-25).
- **Make every effort to live in peace with everyone** *and to be holy; without holiness no one will see the Lord* (12:14).
- **Keep on loving one another as brothers and sisters.** *Do not forget to* **show hospitality to strangers,** *for by so doing some*

people have shown hospitality to angels without knowing it (13:1-2).

Our days of rest should be totally solitary only rarely, I believe. Even those of us who are introverts will usually find that an effort to initiate some time with others enhances our rest.

An Antidote to Conflict

Spending time resting together is also a huge antidote to one of the biggest rest robbers of all time: conflict. Paul notes this effect of conflict in 2 Corinthians 7:5: *For when we came into Macedonia, we had no rest, but we were harassed at every turn—conflicts on the outside, fears within.* Stress in relationships takes its toll on our ability to find our focus in God's goodness, and often turns our eyes back on our own rightness or competence.

There are many ways we can try to deal with conflict, but one of them involves leaning into relaxed, social time together. Years ago, I was in a conflict with a woman on our team, and as a result, I avoided her. But instead of making the conflict better, it actually made it worse. In my mind, she grew more and more into a negative caricature of herself, and the conflict grew more insurmountable. It was only when we started spending regular social time together that I was able to see her more positively. This time doesn't necessarily make a conflict go away, but it does create an atmosphere in which it can be addressed and resolved.

Spending recreational time together with family, friends and coworkers to talk and eat and share also can prevent conflict as you gather around common interests and conversations. This is especially true as you attempt to use that time to *encourage one another* and *spur one another on to love and good deeds.* It is one of the big things we can do to *keep on loving one another as brothers and sisters,* and to *make every effort to live at peace with everyone.* And it is one of the primary ingredients of a restful Sabbath day.

Family Time

Speaking of brothers and sisters, one of the most important ingredients we can fill our rest time with is family time. Fewer families make the time to eat together daily any more—but this can be a sacred and significant way to rest. And it can have a significant impact on how your children learn to rest as well.

Studies have shown that it is not a great Sunday School or youth group that most influences children's future devotion to God, but their parents. It is really in the downtime—when they have the chance to hear you talk about your own gratitude to God for his provision, and stories of his redemption and restoration in your life— that they learn to rest in him for themselves. No wonder Deuteronomy 6:6-7 says: *These commandments that I give you today are to be on your hearts. Impress them on your children.* **Talk about them when you sit at home and when you walk along the road, when you lie down and when you get up.**

But family time is not necessarily exclusive time. There are people you can invite to share in your home and family, especially those who have no family near them. Psalm 68:6 says that *God sets the lonely in families.* If you have a family, there are sure to be lonely people that He wishes include in it.

Hospitality sets up a situation where people stop being strangers and start acting as family to each other, at least for that time. When we dedicate part of our resources to inviting others to be part of our inner circle this way, when we give over part of our free time to being with others to enjoy and encourage them, we will find ourselves with brothers and sisters who love us back.

And who knows—as Hebrews 13:2 hints to us, you might just serve Sunday lunch to *an angel without knowing it...*

Reflections:

- 1 Timothy 5:9-10 says, *"No widow may be put on the list of widows unless she is... well known for her good deeds, such as bringing up children, showing hospitality, washing the feet of the Lord's people, helping those in trouble..."* If it were **you** applying to be put on this list for support, would you qualify according to these requirements? Why or why not?

- How have others encouraged you? How do you see yourself *encouraging others*? How would you see this fitting into your free time? How do you think this would help you rest?

- Are you an extravert or an introvert? (That is, does being with other people normally energize or drain you?) If you are an introvert, are there any times you have spent with others that do seem to add to your rest? Why was this? Who were they? How can you learn from and lean into this?

- How does your family figure in to your free time? How could you invite others in to share some of your family time? Do any specific people come to mind?

- Hospitality and eating with others doesn't have to mean a fancy dinner at your house—it could be delivery pizza, or ice cream sundaes, or breakfast pancakes. It doesn't even have to be in your house—you can invite people to your favorite café. How could you invite people into your presence in simple ways?

24 Re-Creation

*So whether you eat or drink or whatever you do, **do it all for the glory of God.*** (1 Corinthians 10:31)

Do you know what you really need to rest well? A new RV!

No, I don't actually mean you should go out and buy a luxury motor home. I mean that you need a new "recreational vehicle," a new way of transporting yourself from being self-reliant on your own entertainment, with decreasing returns on pleasure, to a place where free time starts to "re-create" you—where it really makes you new. You need to climb on board an idea that keeps your leisure activity from turning into something that doesn't actually satisfy your need for rest!

The road trip begins in our minds and our hearts with the verse above: *Do it all for the glory of God.*

Playing in Faith

This is closely related (the flip side, actually) to the idea that we looked at in Chapters 19 & 20, from Romans 14: *Everything that does not come from faith is sin.* Paul was talking in this text about the choices that we make about things that are not specifically prohibited in Scripture, what he calls in v. 1 *"disputable matters."*

This encompasses a great deal of our leisure activity, for there is almost nothing that you could do for fun that someone would not call bad and another good. Eating meat, dancing, watching TV, reading novels, drinking a beer, going to the movies, playing sports, listening to popular music... all of these have been condemned by some other Christian at some time. And then if you add the extra condition of what is acceptable when one is observing a Sabbath day, the question is further confused.

So how do we decide which things are beneficial—truly re-creational—and which are valueless, or even draining?

We have to ask ourselves the question: **Can I do this in faith, enjoying it and thanking God for it? Can I *[insert activity here]* for the glory of God?** If the answer is yes, then go for it! If it is no, then you should reconsider. As Romans 14:6 says, *Whoever eats meat does* *so to the Lord, for they give thanks to God; and whoever abstains does so to the Lord and gives thanks to God.* And in v. 5: *Each of them should be fully convinced in their own mind.*

Of course, we are not talking here about stuff that clearly wrong. We can't steal to God's glory and thank him for it. And even good things can become bad if practiced from selfish motives. As well, many things that could be enjoyed in faith if done in moderation can become bad—draining and deleterious to us—if done in excess. This is why we are warned in Scripture about gluttony and drunkenness.

We have all heard the stories of the experiment in which rats had electrodes planted into the pleasure centres of their brains, which they could activate by pressing a lever. The rats would do this repeatedly, even in preference over food and water, until they would eventually die of exhaustion. People can behave in ways that are not much different. Isaiah confronted this excess, which leads to ignoring what God has done in favour of reliance on our own recreation:

> *Woe to those who rise early in the morning*
> *to run after their drinks,*
> *who stay up late at night till they are inflamed with wine.*
> *They have harps and lyres at their banquets,*
> *pipes and timbrels and wine,*
> **but they have no regard for the deeds of the Lord,**
> **no respect for the work of his hands.** (Isaiah 5:11-12)

We do well to take to heart Ephesians 5:15-18: *Be very careful, then, how you live—**not as unwise but as wise,** making the most of every opportunity, because the days are evil. Therefore **do not be foolish, but understand what the Lord's will is.** Do not get drunk on wine, which leads to debauchery. Instead, be filled with the Spirit...*

Re-Creating Body, Mind, and Soul

Over the last few chapters we have looked at some specific things that can help with our re-creation. Taking time to deliberately refrain from work. Getting enough sleep. Dedicating time to worship, both public and private. Spending time with family and friends. But there are so many other good things that we can also do in faith that can also be re-creational.

One is building up our bodies through exercise. Without it, we will not rest well physically, and are less likely to be focused mentally.

Even Paul, so single-minded, concedes this in 1 Timothy 4:8: **For physical training is of some value,** but godliness has value for all things, holding promise for both the present life and the life to come. Just imagine the advantages if you combined both...

Another is taking in stories and ideas through books, TV, movies, podcasts, and so on. These can feed our minds and make them grow, especially as we keep in mind the principle in Philippians 4:8: *Finally, brothers and sisters, whatever is true, whatever is noble, whatever is right, whatever is pure, whatever is lovely, whatever is admirable—if anything is excellent or praiseworthy—think about such things.* This does not mean we have to read only Christian books or watch Christian movies. God can speak truth to us and recreate our minds through many avenues. (An example: in my marriage, he used a historical novel and a leadership book to convict me about changes I needed to make in how I related to my husband.)

A third (but by no means final) way we might engage in re-creation is to be involved in creativity ourselves. This might include playing a musical instrument, sewing a dress, planting a garden, cooking a meal, planning an event, restoring a car, decorating a room, writing a story... We are all made to be creative in some way, whether practically, intellectually, or artistically; it is part of our reflection of God. When we lose ourselves in leisure activities like these, we get a little taste of what eternity is going to be like, when we will be able to enjoy working without being tired, when in our resurrected bodies we can simultaneously work and rest.

Sabbath Re-Creation

In the post-exilic observance of the Jewish Sabbath, all creative activities on the Sabbath were banned as work. The Jews reasoned that if God rested from creation on the Sabbath, that they should as well. They based their list of 39 prohibitions on the kinds of work that were necessary for constructing the Tabernacle, God's representation of heaven here on Earth.

But I have come to believe that as people living in the New Creation era, observing Sabbath as a prophetic symbol of the coming reality, the kind of creativity that is apart from our normal daily work is quite appropriate on a day of rest set apart to God. We get to **demonstrate and experience a little bit of what it will be like in the City of God, when our rest and work are integrated in the Sabbath that is to come** (see Revelation 21). These activities are not meant to replace the reflection and relationships that define the day, but may supplement them with a kind of re-creation that is beneficial to their purposes.

Think of the connections that could be made here. Going out for a Sunday bike ride, noticing God's creation around you. Watching a TV show with your family, and then talking about how the characters acted in that situation, and how that is like or unlike you. Doing a piece of embroidery on the terrace in an attitude of prayer and meditation, pondering on what you heard and discussed in church.

One caution, however, is that if we are deliberately setting aside a time not to work, but to be in God's presence, we have to make sure that these things have not also become work to us. If I am working on writing a novel in my spare time, that may be the day to lay it aside. If you are training for a marathon or playing on a sports team every day, you might want to reserve that as a rest day. If we are in the process of repainting our house, perhaps the brushes should be downed for that time. A proposal for a rule of thumb: **If it feels like work, it probably is.**

When we set aside Sabbath times and fill them with the things God tells us will give us real rest, things that will cause us to rely less on ourselves and more on him, we can expect that this rest will spill over into the rest of our leisure time—and even into our work. As we do all to the glory of God, everything out of faith and trust in him, then we will begin to find that rather than working hard and resting from exhaustion, that we can start with God's rest and let our work spring from that.

Reflections:

- What are some activities that feel particularly re-creational to you—that feel like they feed your soul?
- What, as you ponder it, are some activities that you use to relax that might not be something you could really do to God's glory, or that you might be doing to excess? What could you do instead of these activities?
- What are some recreational activities that you think would make a good part of a Sabbath day or time? What are some that you think you probably should avoid because they are too much like work?
- Read again Revelation 21-22. Write down your thoughts about what you look forward to about a New Creation time when your work will not be tiring and your rest will not be boring. How can the re-creational things you enjoy doing help you to remember this?

Rest definition #23:
Rest = re-creation

part five:
working restfully

25 Working from Rest

For it is by grace you have been saved, through faith—and this not from yourselves, it is the gift of God— not by works, so that no one can boast. **For we are God's workmanship, created in Christ Jesus to do good works, which God prepared in advance for us to do.** (Ephesians 2:8-10)

"No rest is worth anything except the rest that is earned." That screensaver on my friend's iPad reminded him daily of what was really important in our culture, a statement of our "work hard, play hard" ethos. This is how we usually think about the relationship between rest and work: Rest is something you earn as a reward for hard work, when you have finished the task you are supposed to do.

Of course, this concept causes a problem when your work is never done, and you just keep on working... and working... with no reward in sight. Or when the time you do eventually take off makes you feel guilty, knowing that there is still a lot left to do. Or when it seems like your work is so mind-numbingly boring and exhausting that you could never rest enough from it.

Rest Before Work

Over the last several chapters, we have considered the idea of a day of rest—the "one day in seven" mentioned in the Fourth Commandment. But the Commandment also talks about the rest of the week: *Six days you shall labour and do all your work* (Exodus 20:9). Other than the daily disciplines that we looked at already, how does rest relate to these work-filled days?

The answer turns our accepted wisdom on its head. We are not made to work hard and then collapse, but to rest **first**—and then work out of that rest.

Look at the text at this chapter's beginning, reminding us once more that God's work of salvation on our behalf is *the gift of God*. It is not something we earn; it is *not by works, so that no one can boast*. It is complete—just as we have seen God's other works to be, and we can rest in it by faith. But then the verse goes on to talk about us doing *good works*. These are not works that earn our salvation, but that follow and flow out of the rest created by that salvation, and they too are carried out in faith.

And this pattern of resting in God first through faith and working out of rest applies to every work of God, to every area of our lives. As we depend in faith on God's completed works (creation, provision, redemption and renewal), enjoying his provision and presence, then we can do the work to which we are called from this position of rest—instead of out of anxiety, ambition, competition, insecurity, or a search for identity.

Made For Works that were Made For You

God has created each of us uniquely, with a unique purpose and calling here on earth. Each one of us is an unparalleled work of art that God has made—*his workmanship*. You might also translate this word "his masterpiece." You are worthy of being hung on the walls of the finest art museum, so people can marvel at the way God has *fearfully and wonderfully made* you (Psalm 139:14). And this refers not only to your physical body working together in all its intricacy, but also to your unique strengths and preferences, your modes of thinking and learning, your ways of relating to people and accomplishing things.

But in this verse, you are not the only masterpiece He makes. God has also handcrafted a whole series of good works that are just waiting out there for you to do them. Only you can do them, because you were made for them, just as they were for you. You just have to go out and look for them. Your life can be like a treasure hunt, where you can wake up each day with excitement and anticipation of the good works that God has waiting for you!

When we begin to perceive our lives in this way—as a treasure hunt for good works that are already complete in God's finished work of redemption—life becomes an adventure instead of unending labour or boring repetition. We can look for the next good work, waiting around the corner, hiding behind a door, anticipating when we would discover it and carry it out with flying colours.

All Our Works Can Be Good Works

Now when Paul says that we are created to do good works, he is not just talking about helping little old ladies cross the road. He is talking about the whole gamut of our lives, whether that is stocking shelves at the supermarket, or feeding the baby, or untangling an issue of law for a company. Any small thing, any big task—in fact, anything that is not called "sin" in Scripture—can be a "good work," from sweeping the floor to populating a database. The secret is that it is done dedicated to the glory of God, as an act of worship to the Creator who created both you and the work. As I Corinthians 10:31 reminded us: *So whether you eat or drink or whatever you do, do it all for the glory of God.*

As we learn more about ourselves, about the unique talents, gifts and strengths God has endowed us with, we may find clues to the kind of good works that are out there for us. People with a special gift of empathy may find themselves listening to and encouraging others. People with a passion for learning may find themselves teaching. People with a talent for leadership get things moving in directions that can make a difference. This makes the treasure hunt all the more exciting as we learn what we were truly made for!

Whatever your primary job is, whether you are a salaried employee, or a parent at home, or a student, or a volunteer for a charity, you will find it chock full of good works that God has prepared for you. These will include the mundane rituals, like filing papers or washing the dishes, as well as the big things, like serving customers, helping a child, or running a conference. The work that we do—at home, at school, at the office—is part of our calling from God.

This may be obvious if you have a job that is uniquely suited to your strengths and abilities. But it is equally true even if you feel that you have a dead-end job, one you took simply to keep body and soul together! What better way to liven up a job flipping burgers than to see it as one more scene of the on-going treasure hunt for custom-made good works that only you can carry out? (Think of yourself as an undercover good-work commando...)

Doing Good Works in Bad Ways

The problem arises when we do these "good works" in bad ways—when we fail to rest first in God's completed works, and think that our work is all about us. We rely on ourselves, thinking that whatever important is accomplished, we must do. Or we see ourselves as the sole beneficiaries of our works, doing them to lay up treasure on earth rather than treasure in heaven, whether that is financial treasure or the treasure of praise and reputation. When we fail to rest first, our own agendas, drives, or fears become the catalyst for our work, rather than the glory and enjoyment of God as his particular purpose for us shines out in our lives.

And as we cease to work from rest, our work—whether our paid job or something we do to prove ourselves worthy—becomes more and more tiring. We worry more about what we have not gotten done. We strive to tick more off our lists. We find our work deadening instead of life-enhancing. We distract ourselves with various leisure pursuits, wondering why we are still so tired.

Isaiah 64:6 tells us what good works look like when they come from self-effort: *All of us have become like one who is unclean, and all our righteous acts are like filthy rags.* (Please forgive my explanation here its forthrightness, but here goes...) The term *"filthy rags"* here is talking about menstrual cloths. For me to be conceited about my own self-righteous efforts is as ridiculous as for me to proudly show you what goes in my bathroom wastebasket once a month. Self-righteous pride is disgusting!

The *good works that he has prepared for us to do* are really not our own. When Christ finished his work of redemption, he did not only forgive us our sins, but he gave us his righteousness. The works created for us are part of this righteousness, which is why they are perfectly acceptable to God, and not like filthy rags.

We do not make these works; we only step into them as they cross our path. Because in reality, since they are works of God, they are also complete like all his other works, ready for us to discover them. Anything that interrupts us on the job—why, it just might be another good work that we had not anticipated, knocking at our door. And anything we do not get done—that we wanted to complete but were unable—we can trust to God as well, for all that is good is already complete in him.

My friend has changed his screen saver. He doesn't have to earn his rest any more, but instead knows that he can rest first in Christ's works as they are retooled specially for him to carry out here on earth.

Reflections:

Rest Definition #24:
Rest ≠ finishing all my work first

- What do you normally have to do to feel like you have earned a rest or break? What do you think it would look like for you to rest first—to work from a position of rest? What would change?
- Do any of these attitudes impact your work: anxiety, ambition, competition, insecurity, or a lack of identity? How would working out of rest make that different?
- What are the factors in your life that cause your work (whether in your job, at home, in serving others, or wherever) to lose life and become deadening to you (overload, competition, anxiety, boredom, etc.)? How could these be changed by a perspective of faith?
- What does it mean to you to know that God has uniquely gifted you to accomplish particular things in your life? What does it mean to know that he has already prepared good works out there for you to do? That all you have to do is look for them? How does this change what you do practically—how you handle interruptions, routine tasks, unexpected setbacks and so on?

Rest Definition #25:
Rest = finding good works God has prepared for me

26 Laziness vs. Rest

*We hear that some among you are idle. They are not busy; they are busybodies. Such people we command and urge in the Lord Jesus Christ to settle down and earn the bread they eat. And as for you, brothers, **never tire of doing what is right.** (2 Thessalonians 3:11-13)*

We do not want you to become lazy, but to imitate those who through faith and patience inherit what has been promised. (Hebrews 6:12)

We have thought quite a bit so far about workaholics: those who cannot quite believe that their work is not the most important thing in the world. We have seen that this is a form of self-reliance that sees our own security, accomplishment and identity as "all up to me." And quite rightly, we have identified this as the opposite of rest.

But some of us don't really have a problem with overworking—we seem to rest quite a lot. We watch a lot of TV; we leave work early; we "take a break" to play a computer game—only to discover that we are still playing an hour and a half later. Or maybe we feel that we work quite hard when we are at the job, but when we are off, our time is our own—and anyone who asks us to do anything will be met with indignant refusal. Does this mean we have mastered the art of resting?

The Selfish Sluggard

The book of Proverbs would say no. It is full of quotes about this, calling the lazy person a "sluggard"—a word reminiscent of the phlegmy creatures one finds creeping up the garden path! Here are a few samples:

- *As a door turns on its hinges, so a sluggard turns on his bed. (26:14)*
- *The sluggard buries his hand in the dish; he is too lazy to bring it back to his mouth. (26:15)*
- *The sluggard craves and gets nothing, but the desires of the diligent are fully satisfied. (13:4)*
- *Sluggards do not plough in season; so at harvest time they look but find nothing. (20:4)*

We can see from all of this that laziness and rest are nowhere near the same thing. The end of laziness is unsatisfied craving. Just as the workaholic is self-centred in thinking that it is all up to him, so the lazy person centres his/her own life on the satisfaction of his own appetites. He has convinced himself that he deserves to be supported or compensated by others in some way. She is positive that all of her time is hers, and that she deserves to spend it how she chooses. These are lies, but part of the reason why Proverbs says: *The sluggard is wiser in his own eyes than seven men who answer discreetly* (26:16).

Laziness fails to recognize God as Creator, and instead sees the world as "mine." My time is mine, my stuff is mine, my needs predominate. I will provide for those appetites (or get others to) no matter what because I deserve it. The world is mine to consume as I wish.

The Man Who Will Not Work

All of this goes against the two purposes of work that we will look at in more detail later: working with God in provision and renewal. Paul wrote to the Thessalonians about *idle people*, in the text quoted at the beginning of the chapter. These people somehow felt entitled that others would provide for them, rather than working with God for the provision of their own needs. Apparently these were able-bodied people, with nothing preventing them from working, for in a proverb of his own, Paul says, *"If a man will not work, he shall not eat"* (2 Thessalonians 2:10).

These passages, of course, are not referring to those who through no fault of their own are unable to work, through loss of health or loss of a job, through discrimination or misfortune. The Old Testament Israelites were warned by the prophets over and over that these people must be protected and supported, and condemned for taking advantage of the *widows and orphans*. In the early Church it is clear that caring for such people was a major ministry (see Acts 6:1-7). And Paul urges his protégé: *Give proper recognition to those widows who are really in need* (I Timothy 5:3).

But even those who through various circumstances are prevented from holding remunerative jobs are not to live lives of laziness, sponging off the handouts of others. Paul says further: *No widow may be put on the list of widows unless she... is well known for her good deeds, such as bringing up children, showing hospitality, washing the feet of the Lord's people, helping those in trouble and devoting herself to all kinds of good deeds* (I Timothy 5:9-10).

Even those who are dependent on the charity of others have contributions that they may make to our community. In our volunteer organization, we have seen asylum seekers (who are prevented by law from working) find purpose by volunteering with us to help others in need. We all, no matter what our employment status, have *good works* that God has created specifically for us to do! By participating in these, we demonstrate our reliance on God rather than our entitlement to being supported by others' labour. If we would receive God's provision, we must prove ourselves willing to participate in his works. As the verse at the beginning of the chapter reminds us, we are to *never tire of doing right.*

Destruction vs. Re-Creation

More subtle than refusing altogether to work is the kind of laziness in which people do the minimum to earn their pay, and prefer their own recreation to the "re-creation" that God calls us to in our work. They labour half-heartedly, preferring to spend their time and energy on their own appetites and desires. They are consumers of creation rather than renewers of it.

As a result, things decay and go downhill: *Through laziness, the rafters sag; because of idle hands, the house leaks* (Ecclesiastes 10:18). A particularly disturbing proverb tells us: **One who is slack in his work is brother to one who destroys** (18:9). Laziness is not just doing nothing—it is the very opposite of renewal. **It is actually destruction!**

Laziness can take many different forms:

- Procrastination
- Avoidance of unpleasant/difficult activities
- Letting other people do what you could/should do
- Taking on as little as possible
- Taking more time off than you are due
- Doing jobs halfway
- Abandoning projects when bored
- Oversleeping
- Addictions (including TV, computer, games, food and more)
- Lack of relational initiative or response
- Overprotection of "personal time"
- A sense that you deserve things from those around you

This list just begins to scratch the surface, but maybe you recognize yourself in one or two of these (as I do)...

Empty Counterfeits of Rest

The crazy thing is that all this "rest" does not satisfy our souls. It only creates a craving that becomes more and more empty the more time we take off, the more we sleep in, the longer we play the video game, the more we drink, the more we avoid tasks, the less we work. It is a substitute for the kind of rest God offers, which spends "time off" in his presence and the presence of others, focusing on him as the Giver of rest.

As we have noted several times before, this does not mean that we cannot sleep in or watch a TV show. These things done to God's glory are also good works! But when we rely on them to build us up, when we suck them dry to sate our drive for pleasure, when we attempt to push the same button over and over to make ourselves feel good—that is the road to emptiness.

Proverbs says it again:

> The craving of a sluggard will be the death of him,
>   because his hands refuse to work.
> All day long he craves for more,
>   but the righteous give without sparing. (21:25-26)

Here is the paradox—those who live to consume only want more, while those who give are blessed.

Jesus told a parable about three servants given bags of gold to invest for their master while he was on a journey in Matthew 25. The first invests his five bags and makes five more; the second invests his two bags and makes two more. The master is pleased with both men. The last servant, with one bag of gold, buries it in the ground and makes excuses as to why he has not made anything with it. The master calls him a "wicked, lazy servant" and throws him out.

We also are given a great wealth—abilities, talents, resources, gifts, skills—to be used for God's purposes here in the world. We must not bury such wealth through laziness. Jesus says, "From everyone who has been given much, much will be demanded; and from the one who has been entrusted with much, much more will be asked" (Luke 12:48). Let us choose to be participants in his God's purposes, carrying out his eternally complete works!

Reflections:

Rest Definition #26:
Rest ≠ laziness

- In what areas do you struggle with laziness? (Look at the bullet-pointed list in the chapter if you need help thinking about this!)
- What excuses do you usually use for laziness? How do you justify it? Have you ever experienced an increase in tiredness directly because of laziness? What happened? Why do you think this was?
- Why do you think God gives such strong warnings about laziness? Why does it not end up meeting our need for rest?
- If you are currently without work—not through laziness but through some other circumstance—what are some of the works that God may be calling you to pursue during this time? (Some ideas: pursuing job opportunities, helping care for family members or others in need, developing new skills through study or rehabilitation, volunteering with your church or an organization…) How can you show gratitude to those God has sent to provide for you in this time?

27 Working with God in Provision

The Lord God took the man and put him in the Garden of Eden to work it and take care of it. And the Lord God commanded the man, "You are free to eat from any tree in the garden..." (Genesis 2:15-16)

Birds in cages have easy, but boring, lives. Every morning the cover comes off the cage. The water bottle is refilled. Seeds are put in the little tray. Once a week or so, the newspaper at the bottom is changed. Everything is taken care of for them. (Too bad they can't fly.)

We have looked at the importance of resting in God's provision and redemption as the basis for any real rest. But this may lead to the question: if God is going to provide anyway, what is the point of my work?

Contrary to what some may think, work is not the result of the curse on Adam after his rebellion. Even before the fall, God had given the first couple a meaningful part in tending his creation, as we can see in the verse above. God never intended for us to be blobs sitting in floating chairs with every need at hand, like the bloated humans in the movie *Wall-E*. Rather, he involves us with him in the on-going aspects of his work—as we continue to trust that he has taken care of the bottom line.

Meaningful Participation in Provision

Right at the beginning, God involves people in his work of provision, as they would take care of the garden and gather food for themselves. Even after the Fall, God says that although now work would become more difficult, Adam would still have the possibility to provide for himself and his family through his farming. This ability to continue to work with God in his provision was a grace God gave people even in the midst of the curse. Work would continue to be meaningful in their lives.

We can see the relationship between God's provision and man's work in Psalm 104:27-28:

> All creatures look to you
> to give them their food at the proper time.

> *When you give it to them,*
>   *they gather it up;*
>   *when you open your hand,*
>   *they are satisfied with good things.*

God is the giver; we are the gatherers. We saw this as well in the Exodus 16 story about God giving manna to the Israelites, as he gave them miraculous food, and they gathered it in.

Giving and gathering: God has given us the privilege to be co-labourers with him in his great work of Provision, already complete in eternity, but worked out day by day. This is as true for us now as with was for our First Parents. Even though our work may sometimes be frustrating, boring or difficult, it gains meaning in part because we are able to provide the needs of ourselves and our families, resting our ultimate reliance on God. We are not like caged birds waiting for our owner to dump seed in the little tray. We are free people, playing an important and responsible role in God's work of provision.

When we pray, "Give us this day our daily bread," we recognize God as giver. We also recognize that we are not entitled to gross surplus, like the rich man in the Jesus' parable who wanted to build bigger barns, but only to our daily needs being met.

Provision for the Daily Needs of Others

In fact, the plural pronouns in the Lord's Prayer remind us that we do not pray only for our **own** daily needs to be met, but also for the needs of those around us ("Give **us** this day... "). And so, if God has somehow provided us with a surplus, he has also provided us with the means to become the answer to our own prayer! Those of us who are rich (i.e. any who have more than their daily needs taken care of) are part of God's answer to our question when we ask Him: *What about those whose needs are not being met?*

There are those who, through disability, persecution, or misfortune have lost the ability to provide for themselves, temporarily or permanently. They might live near you, or they might live on another continent. If you are a person who has more than daily bread, one of the *good works* that God is very likely calling you to do is to share with those who have none, to be his agent of provision in this world. (If they are in your own family, then you are **definitely** called to help provide for them--see I Timothy 5:8 for some very strong words on this subject.)

The Hebrew Christians were commended for standing *side by side with those* who *were publicly exposed to insult and persecution* (Hebrews 10:33); this would have included feeding them in jail and providing for their families.   The writer further asked them to *continue to remember those in prison as if you were together with them in prison, and those who are mistreated as if you yourselves were suffering* (13:3). How can we ignore those in need around us when we are not suffering persecution as the Hebrew Christians were, but enjoying excess?

Generosity to Spread the Gospel

In addition, our surplus can be the means for providing for those whom God has called to carry the Gospel to various parts of the world. Paul often worked as a tentmaker to support himself on his missions, but he insisted that he and other Gospel-bearers had the right to support from those in the Body of Christ:

> *Don't you know that those who serve in the temple get their food from the temple, and that those who serve at the altar share in what is offered on the altar? In the same way, the Lord has commanded that those who preach the gospel should receive their living from the gospel.* (1 Corinthians 9:13-14)

This also means that those whom God has called into full-time Christian ministry should not be embarrassed about being supported by those who have other callings. They can be up front about their needs before their brothers and sisters, neither greedy nor grovelling. They have been called to rest in God's provision in a way that, hopefully, will remind them with every paycheck of how God works together with people to accomplish his purposes. And they should recognize thankfully both God's provision and people's generosity, as Paul did with the Philippians: *I am amply supplied, now that I have received... the gifts you sent. They are a fragrant offering, an acceptable sacrifice, pleasing to God* (Philippians 4:18).

Our Work In Itself Provides for Others

Not only can we be generous to others from the money that we earn by our labour, but our work itself may intrinsically help provide resources for the needs of people, as we provide goods and services for them, or as we care for others in various roles. In being a nurse, you provide care for those in need of health and help. In being a teacher, you provide instruction and training for children who are growing up, skills and knowledge to interact with their world. In being an IT repair guy, you provide people with the tools and the information they need to do their work well, and to connect with each other. Knowing what it is that we are doing to provide for others through our work can help us connect more closely each day in joy to our God, as we participate each day in his work of provision.

We can also choose to participate in ministry or volunteer work that seeks directly to meet the needs of others. We have seen many people that do not feel this sense of working directly with God in provision find purpose in volunteering with our organization to do things like serving a meal to homeless people at a train station, or sharing coffee and conversation with elderly people at a hospital. The more closely we are tied in to God's purposeful works in the world, the more of a sense of purpose we will find in our own lives, and the more "restful" our work will be.

Faith-Filled Generosity

Being an agent of God's generous provision to others means believing that he will take care of your own needs—that you do not have to "build bigger barns" and save up more and more just to be safe. Your work is not the **source** of provision—it is just one **means** that God uses. If you lost your job, if your house burned down, if you became a quadriplegic, God could still provide for you. And it would likely be through other people! In order to work from rest and be able to participate fully with God in his work of provision, we must believe this.

But perhaps it is in stepping out in faith-filled generosity and working with God in providing for the needs of others beyond our own that we see that his provision is limitless and faithful. As we see him provide through us, we are reassured, as the generous Philippians were, that *my God will meet all your needs according to the riches of his glory in Christ Jesus* (Phil 4:19).

Reflections:

Think about the work that you do, not only in your job, but also in other arenas such as home, ministry, and volunteer service.

- What are some ways that you see that God is using you as an agent of his provision (for yourself and others)?
- Are there any ways in which your daily work is intrinsically providing something to others that they need (food, care, communication, help, direction, information, etc.)? How does this impact how you think about your job?
- What makes you nervous about being generous with others? Are you worried that you won't have enough for yourself or that you won't have a big enough safety net? That people will take advantage of you? Or is it simply a desire for more "stuff" than you really need? What changes is God calling you to make in your attitude towards God's provision for you through your work?
- How might you participate with God in providing for those in need? What kind of "good work" is he preparing for you? Is it a needy family in your church? A ministry to the homeless or refugees in your city? A development initiative overseas, such as funding a well in a poor community so that agriculture can thrive, water-borne diseases reduced, and less time spent seeking water? Pray about how God might have you participate in this way.
- How can you participate with God in providing for those called into Christian ministry? Is there anyone you know in particular that you feel a connection to and would like to support?
- If God is calling you into full-time ministry, is the financial support of others an issue for you? Do you believe that he can provide for you in this way? What attitudes do you need to cultivate in order to avoid being either grovelling or greedy in relating to supporters?

Rest definition #27:
Rest = work as the means, not the source, of provision

28 Lessons from the Sabbatical Year

*The Lord said to Moses at Mount Sinai, "...When you enter the land I am going to give you, the land itself must observe a sabbath to the Lord. For six years sow your fields, and for six years prune your vineyards and gather their crops. **But in the seventh year the land is to have a year of sabbath rest, a sabbath to the Lord.** Do not sow your fields or prune your vineyards. Do not reap what grows of itself or harvest the grapes of your untended vines. The land is to have a year of rest."* (Leviticus 25:1-5)

How would you like to take a year off once every seven years? Sounds relaxing, doesn't it? When I first ran across this commandment, I thought, "Lucky Israelites! Must be nice!"

Of course, there is a sound agricultural principle behind this commandment. Land that is planted year after year with the same crops becomes depleted of nutrients. Having a year to lie fallow allows the land to recover some of its fertility. But there is far more to the Sabbatical year than soil conservation...

Feeding the Poor, Eating the Surplus

During this seventh year, the people of Israel were instructed not only that they must not **plant** their fields, but also that they must not **reap** what came up voluntarily, or fruited on their vines. This food was for another purpose: *"For six years you are to sow your fields and harvest the crops, but during the seventh year let the land lie unploughed and unused. **Then the poor among your people may get food from it,** and the wild animals may eat what is left. Do the same with your vineyard and your olive grove"* (Exodus 23:10-11). The poor—who were allowed to glean around the edges of the fields in normal years—were allowed in this year to reap everything that came up.

Which raised the question: where would the landowners get **their** food during this seventh year? God had anticipated just such a question: *You may ask, "What will we eat in the seventh year if we do not plant or harvest our crops?" I will send you such a blessing in the sixth year that the land will yield enough for three years. While you* *plant during the eighth year, you will eat from the old crop and will continue to eat from it until the harvest of the ninth year comes in* (Leviticus 25:20-22).   God promises a bumper crop that they can eat from in the Sabbatical year, until the next year's harvest.

Forgiving Debts, Releasing Slaves

But that was not all that was to happen during this Sabbatical year. Two other big things were going on:

- *At the end of every seven years* **you must cancel debts.** *This is how it is to be done: Every creditor shall cancel any loan they have made to a fellow Israelite. They shall not require payment from anyone among their own people, because the Lord's time for cancelling debts has been proclaimed.* (Deuteronomy 15:1-2)
- *If any of your people—Hebrew men or women—sell themselves to you and serve you six years, in the seventh year* **you must let them go free.** (Deuteronomy 15:12)

It seems that I got the wrong perspective on this "vacation year" the first time round! This year off doesn't look so "lucky" for the landowners, those who are rich. They can't eat from their fields or vines or orchards. They have to forgive the debts people owe them. And they have to let their servants go. It sounds like a good year if you were poor! But if you had much, obeying these commandments might seem like loss and worry!

And then, in addition, God gives instructions like this for releasing your servants: *And when you release them, do not send them away empty-handed.* **Supply them liberally** *from your flock, your threshing floor and your winepress.* **Give to them as the Lord your God has blessed you** (Deuteronomy 15:13-14). More profit down the drain!

God is the Owner—Who Blesses Generosity

God wanted the Israelites to know that the land that they thought of as "theirs" was really his. And because it was his, he would care for it, and not allow them to exploit it by farming it to death. The people, too—debtors and employees—must not be seen in their relation to creditors and masters, but as fellow Israelites, people of God. The money they owed, the work they performed, was not something that could be "owned."

And God also wanted them to know for sure that it was not their own work that was the source of provision for their needs, but Him. He gives them every assurance that obedience would **not** result in loss, but in blessing:

- *Follow my decrees and be careful to obey my laws, and you will live safely in the land. Then the land will yield its fruit, and **you will eat your fill and live there in safety.*** (Leviticus 25:18-19)
- *Give generously to [the poor] and do so without a grudging heart; then **because of this the Lord your God will bless you in all your work** and in everything you put your hand to.* (Deuteronomy 15:10)
- *Do not consider it a hardship to set your servant free, because their service to you these six years has been worth twice as much as that of a hired hand. And the Lord your God will **bless you in everything you do.*** (Deuteronomy 15:18)

God was teaching his people a sort of radical rest in this Sabbatical year—a rest that required complete trust that God's promises were true, that he would do as he had said. This rest required the rich not just to hunker down and get through it, but to be open-handed and generous to their less fortunate neighbours, acting as God's source of provision in their need.

The saddest thing is: they almost never did it. It was too hard to *make the effort to enter this rest.* And the time that they spent in captivity—seventy years—was one year for each Sabbath year they had failed to observe. For God had told them that if they failed to obey these commandments: *Then the land will enjoy its sabbath years all the time that it lies desolate and you are in the country of your enemies; then the land will rest and enjoy its sabbaths. All the time that it lies desolate, the land will have the rest it did not have during the sabbaths you lived in it* (Leviticus 26:34-35).

Radically Resting in God's Provision

So what does this have to do with us? Should we take off one year of every seven and live on what we have? How can we apply what God was trying to teach the Israelites?

Most of us reading this are the rich of this world. We are quick to think of the possessions we have as "ours," the result of our own hard work. We forget that we are simply stewards, holding this property in trust for the real Owner, to invest for his purposes. We forget who is the source of our blessings.

We can be radically generous as we radically rest in Him. God told his people, "*There will always be poor people in the land. Therefore I command you to be open-handed toward your fellow Israelites who are poor and needy in your land*" (Deut. 15:11).

We are not exempt from this command. James reminds us in the New Testament, "*What good is it, my brothers and sisters, if someone claims to have faith but has no deeds? Can such faith save them? Suppose a brother or a sister is without clothes and daily food. If one of you says to them, 'Go in peace; keep warm and well fed,' but does nothing about their physical needs, what good is it?*" (James 2:14-16) The quality of our rest in God will be revealed in the quality of our generosity.

But there may also be a time element here. Perhaps God is calling you to take some time off your regular job to help a mission in another country, or to assist a ministry in your town. Perhaps he is calling you to live on the savings he has allowed you to accumulate, or to depend on support from others, as you do this. Perhaps he is asking you to invest your retirement years, or some of it, in his purposes in the world, rather than golf and lunches out.

Every year is meant to be a Sabbath kind of year as we depend on the mercy of God for his provision for us—and pass those blessings on to those around us who are in need of mercy.

Reflections:

- Put yourself in the shoes of a rich Israelite landowner coming up on the Sabbatical year. What would make you want to ignore this commandment? What beliefs would you have to cling to in order for the year to be a joy to you? How might the year become restful to you?
- Meditate again on this verse from Psalm 127:1-2 that we looked at earlier:

  Unless the Lord builds the house,
    the builders labour in vain.
  Unless the Lord watches over the city,
    the guards stand watch in vain.
  In vain you rise early
    and stay up late, toiling for food to eat...

  How does this relate to the principles of the Sabbatical year? How does it impact how you see your work?
- Do you perceive yourself as rich or poor? Do you feel like God has blessed you? How does this impact how you feel about being generous with others?
- Do you tend to look at what you have (and who you have) as belonging to yourself, or to God? How would it make a difference to see yourself as a steward of God's resources?
- What would be your response if God called you to a "sabbatical time," stepping out in faith to spend time not in working to provide for yourself, but to do something bold for him? What could you see yourself doing?

Rest definition #28:
Rest ≠ having enough hoarded resources

Rest definition #29:
Rest = trusting God's blessing by being generous

29 Working with God in Renewal

Now may the God of peace, who through the blood of the eternal covenant brought back from the dead our Lord Jesus, that great Shepherd of the sheep, equip you with everything good for doing his will... (Hebrews 13:20-21)

> What kind of world do you want?
> Think anything...
> Let's start at the start, build a masterpiece
> Be careful what you wish for—history starts now.
> *--Five for Fighting, "World"*

If you listen to popular radio, you will occasionally hear, in between the love jingles and the dance music, songs of longing like the one above. It asks us to consider our responsibility in making the world a better place, and reflects the earnest desire in the heart of every person for a world with *no more death or mourning or crying or pain* (Revelation 21:4). The difference for us as believers in Jesus is that we know that it is not only possible for the world to become this "masterpiece"—it is inevitable as his New Creation is revealed.

Renewal in the Midst of Ruin

This renewal is happening even now. However, this doesn't mean the whole world will get better and better until one day we wake up and the New Heavens and Earth are shining outside our door. Actually, Jesus predicted that many evil and difficult things will happen as the restoration at the end of time draws nearer:

> *"You will hear of wars and rumours of wars, but see to it that you are not alarmed. Such things must happen, but the end is still to come. Nation will rise against nation, and kingdom against kingdom. There will be famines and earthquakes in various places... At that time many will turn away from the faith and will betray and hate each other, and many false prophets will appear and deceive many people"* [Matthew 24:6-7, 10-11].

So how is it, exactly, that God can claim, "I am making everything new"? Because **he begins with us, with his children, and that**

renewal spreads from us out to the whole cosmos. Romans 8:19-21 says, *"For the creation waits in eager expectation for the children of God to be revealed… For the creation itself will be liberated from its bondage to decay and brought into the freedom and glory of the children of God."* **We**, as Ephesians 2:10 reminded us, **are his masterpiece**, individually and collectively.

We are the first examples of the renewal that the whole cosmos is groaning for. We have been reconciled to God, given the righteousness of Jesus, inhabited by the Holy Spirit, who is renewing us daily as we walk in step with him, in the power of Jesus' resurrection. This is the basis of the blessing from Hebrews at the beginning of this chapter. This is the hope of all creation. One day our bodies, subject to disease and disfigurement and decay, will be resurrected and made perfect along with our universe, and death and sin will be banished.

So what, you may ask, does this have to do with my daily work? Everything.

Demonstrating Prophetic Renewal

When Jesus came into the world, he came proclaiming, "Repent, for the kingdom of heaven is near." Then he demonstrated what that new kingdom would look like by healing all who were sick and oppressed. This was not a complete renewal—these people would eventually die—but it was a foretaste of the time when sickness and pain and mourning would be a thing of the past. And then, he sent out his disciples to do the same thing. (You can read about this in Luke 9 and 10.)

We, as disciples of this coming kingdom, are also **called in our work to be agents of renewal, prophetic proclaimers of the coming kingdom.** This prophetic aspect can imbue many of our simplest actions with meaning.

When you clean mildew off the shower wall, do it as an agent of God's renewal, demonstrating what the world will be like when all is made new. When you file papers in their correct places, do it as a prophet of the time when chaos will no longer be allowed to reign. When you pull weeds in a garden, do it as an artist painting a picture of the coming beauty that will be. When you write a scholarly paper on the physical properties of glacial ice, do it to reveal how God has not allowed all on earth to be ruined by evil, but has left beauty and order to be discovered by people as a sign of what was, and what will be.

Sin has brought entropy and decay and death into the world. When we fight these things in any way, mindful of the significance of our actions, we acknowledge the coming kingdom. And when we create beauty and order and harmony, or reveal the hand of God through our discoveries about the world around us, we may consciously act as prophets of this restoration.

Renewal in Relationships

But nowhere is this more evident than in relationships with people. Our own renewal has given us the chance to be an agent of renewal among those around us. 2 Corinthians 5:16-19 says it superbly:

> So from now on **we regard no one from a worldly point of view.** Though we once regarded Christ in this way, we do so no longer. Therefore, **if anyone is in Christ, the new creation has come: The old has gone, the new is here!** All this is from God, who reconciled us to himself through Christ and **gave us the ministry of reconciliation:** that God was reconciling the world to himself in Christ, not counting people's sins against them. And he has committed to us the message of reconciliation.

Co workers, neighbours, clients, family members... we used to look at them from *a worldly point of view.* They were people there to do something for us (admire us, love us, help us, etc.) or that were in our way as antagonists or obstacles. Everyone was evaluated in their relationship to **me.** But now, we see everyone in their relationship to God, who has given us the ministry of reconciliation. They are people for whom Christ died, and that makes us see them differently. They are people who can be permanently renewed right now! As Paul says, *"Christ's love compels us, because we are convinced that one died for all..."* (2 Corinthians 5:14)

So how does this change your interactions with those around you? Those you serve on your job: your boss, your clients, your colleagues? Those you serve in your home: your spouse, your roommates, your children? Those you encounter in your environment: the guy who cuts you off in traffic, the beggar on the street, the smelly guy on the tram? Are you an agent of reconciliation, or rejection? Do you see them as Christ sees them, or only in relationship to your own advantages?

Agents of Reconciliation

First and foremost, we can be agents of reconciliation of others to God. You may do this simply by being open about what God has done for you and is doing for you daily. If you are resting in his provision and renewal in your life, you will have plenty of thankful stories to tell! And your own sense of peace and rest, your lack of anxiety and competition, will cause those who work and live with you to want to know your secret.

But you can also be an agent of reconciliation between people. This begins with yourself, as you daily forgive others like God forgave you. He has not held your massive debts to him against you—why should you think that anyone else owes you anything? We pray for our friends, and for our enemies---one of our most effective tools in this work of renewal. From here we can move into being peacemakers between others who are in conflict as we see each party through God's eyes.

Seeing yourself as an agent of renewal may just transform how you perceive your daily work. But it may also lead you to want to reach out into the world around you, into the hurts of your city, to prophetically proclaim God's renewal in places of darkness. This might be in a simple way, like painting the nails of a battered woman in a shelter—proclaiming that in God's kingdom people living in fear can reimagine trust and beauty. Through prophetic actions like these, you proclaim "The kingdom of heaven is near."

In this work, we are equipped by the resurrection power of Jesus, the author of this restoration who has conquered death itself. Read again the benediction at the beginning of this chapter, and let it be said over you...

Reflections:

- Almost every job has some aspect of renewal to it:
  - Something that is created
  - Something that is ordered
  - Something that is connected
  - Something that is revealed
  - Something that is repaired
  - Something that is restored

  What about your daily work intrinsically demonstrates renewal? How could thinking about it from this perspective transform how you carry it out?

- How could it change your perspective on other people to think that "Christ died for all"? What would change if you thought about others primarily in relation to Christ, rather than primarily in relation to yourself?

- How could you be an agent of reconciliation at your primary place of work? Who does that mean you need to forgive? Between whom are you called to be a peacemaker? (Remember, Matthew 5:9 promises that peacemakers will be called *children of God!*)

- How could you be involved in prophetically showing Christ's coming kingdom to the world in your city or neighbourhood? What issues of justice set your heart on fire? Who are the broken people that you are most drawn to? Don't underestimate the power of small things done in a prophetic way—especially in the company of others. Many people doing small things together makes a big difference!

30 Rest for Your Souls

*"Come to me, all you who are weary and burdened, and I will give you rest. Take my yoke upon you and learn from me, for I am gentle and humble in heart, and **you will find rest for your souls**. For my yoke is easy and my burden is light."* (Matthew 11:28-30)

During the time I have been writing this study, I have listened over and over to a song based on the words above: "Come, All You Weary" by Thrice. And every time I listen to it, I think, "That's for me. I am the weary."

I am so glad Jesus didn't call the strong to himself, those that were able to handle the heavy loads. Rather, he calls those who are burdened, and asks them to trade in a burden they cannot bear for one that they can—a *yoke that is easy and light.*

Jesus' Easy Yoke

It was common in Jesus' time to teach the "Yoke of Torah"—the obligations to the Law of Moses, with each rabbi bringing his own interpretations to it. (A "yoke," in case this word is unfamiliar to you, was a wooden frame for the neck and shoulders, enabling an animal or person to pull or carry a heavy load, such as a plough or water buckets.)

The oral traditions of the scribes and Pharisees had gone far beyond the original demands of Scripture. Jesus talked about the heavy yoke that these teachers put on their followers, when they themselves could not even keep the Commandments perfectly: *Do not do what they do, for they do not practice what they preach. They tie up heavy, cumbersome loads and put them on other people's shoulders, but they themselves are not willing to lift a finger to move them* (Matthew 23:3-4).

Jesus offers his followers something quite different. He does not abolish the Law, but he does interpret it according to its original intent: to love God and others. He points out that sin goes deeper than simply our actions; it is a matter of the heart. He even says, *"Unless your righteousness surpasses that of the Pharisees and the teachers of the law, you will certainly not enter the kingdom of heaven"* (Matthew 5:20).

This does not sound like a lighter burden! But Jesus' yoke is not lighter because he has lower standards—it is lighter because he shares it with us, and takes all the weight.

- He has taken on himself the penalty for all our sins, so that all we need do is confess them to know forgiveness. We do not have to make up or atone for what we have done—he has done that for all time.
- He has given us his own record of righteousness, and created good works out of that righteousness specially crafted for us to do. We do not need to try to impress God with our actions—he is pleased with all that we do in his name, because it is stamped with Christ's perfection.
- He lives with us and in us by his Holy Spirit, guiding and directing us, *delivering us from evil.* We do not have to wonder what we must do or which way to go—he is close beside us, urging us to keep in step with him.

This is the yoke that is easy and light: to stay connected each moment to Jesus, trusting and following him. Rest is not simply a matter of enough sleep, a better-managed schedule or a day off a week—or even observing a Sabbath. It is a daily, moment-by-moment faith that rests on Jesus—on his completed works and on his constant presence.

To do this, we must *learn from him,* and the thing that we must learn is his character: *for I am gentle and humble in heart.* This is the opposite of the self-reliance, of disbelief and hardness of heart. Instead, it is trusting him with the faith of a little child, putting our hand in his as we walk along the road. It is enjoying his presence, and his gifts to us in his presence, and the works we do in his presence. It is being open and generous to those around us, encouraging them and being God's means of provision and renewal to them as others are to us.

Don't Go Back to the Weariness of Self-Effort

Avram, and the community to which the letter of Hebrews was written, were ready to abandon this yoke and go back to the yoke they had known previously. But as Paul also reminded the Galatians, *"It is for freedom that Christ has set us free. Stand firm, then, and do* not let yourselves be burdened again by a yoke of slavery" (Galatians 5:1). When the apostles were considering which of the Laws should be required for the new Gentile converts, Peter said to them: "Why do you try to test God by putting on the necks of Gentiles a yoke that neither we nor our ancestors have been able to bear? No! We believe it is through the grace of our Lord Jesus that we are saved, just as they are" (Acts 15:10-11).

This was also the concern of the writer to the Hebrews for his audience as he wrote to them: Since the promise of entering his rest still stands, let us be careful that none of you be found to have fallen short of it (Hebrews 4:1). Why should they exchange the light yoke of Christ's grace for the heavy one of trying to prove themselves worthy through their own efforts?

It is only when we recognize that we are weary, that we are worn out with the effort of shouldering all our own burdens, that we have a chance of finding the humility of coming to Christ and taking on his yoke instead. It means giving up self-interest—and yet we are promised that following him **is** in our best interest. It means renouncing our appetites—and yet as his delights become ours, we find that instead of unsatisfied craving, the desires of our heart are fulfilled (Psalm 37:4).

We don't have to wait for any special time to rest. We don't have to wait until circumstances are favourable to be able to be at peace. We don't have to stop our work to relax our hearts. At any time, we can turn toward the one who promises to give us rest for our souls.

> Let the beloved of the Lord rest secure in him,
>   for he shields him all day long,
>   and the one the Lord loves rests between his shoulders.
> (Deuteronomy 33:12)

Let us heed today the voice of the writer to the Hebrews:
There remains, then, a Sabbath-rest for the people of God; for anyone who enters God's rest also rests from their works, just as God did from his. Let us, therefore, make every effort to enter that rest... (Hebrews 4:9-11).

Reflections:

- Look back at the first chapter and the ways that you noted weariness in your own life. Over the course of this study, what are some of the antidotes that you have seen to your weariness?
- Write down for yourself a statement of what you need to believe about God and his completed work in order to combat your weariness.
- Look at the next page ("Resolutions to Rest"). What practices or disciplines would help you in making the effort to enter Christ's rest? Pray about how God wants you to make this concrete in your daily life.
- Write a prayer to express your trust in Jesus as you, the weary, come to him for rest.

Rest definition #30:
Rest = depending continually on Jesus

Epilogue: Resolutions to Rest

Be at rest once more, O my soul, for the Lord has been good to you.
(Psalm 116:7)

Here are some suggestions of things you can do to "*make every effort to enter his rest*":

- Make a list of all the ways you can think of the God has provided for you and blessed you, and ways he has worked in your life. Put it where you can see it so that you will be encouraged to have faith in times that you are tempted to rely on your own resources. Memorize the verse above and repeat it often!

- Set aside a time each day to reflect on God and enjoy his presence. Remember this is not something you do so that God will approve of you, but something you do **because** he approves of you. Maybe this is through "praying the office" each day, or a daily Bible reading plan, or devotions with your family or spouse. The vital thing is to focus your thoughts on Him.

- Make sure you are getting the physical rest you need. This might be by going to bed a bit earlier, or by exercising more so that your body is better able to sleep. Or it might be by actually taking a day off work every week, so that you are not constantly working. (Even if your job is ongoing—like being the mother of little kids—you can find ways to limit what you do one day a week by cooking ahead/going out to eat, having your spouse share some responsibilities, or doing special things with your family you wouldn't otherwise do.)

- Figure out what habits or addictions you have that are robbing you of rest (whether physical or psychological) and find a person or group who can help you to work on overcoming them. These may be either lazy habits or compulsive habits.

- Take time off each week to serve as your Sabbath. Find a concentrated time during this day to spend time reflecting on God in a way that is energizing for you. This might be a walk in the woods, a discussion with friends, reading a book that helps you understand God better, drawing/writing/

singing/listening to music, praying aloud, or some other way that you feel connected with God. Really use this time to worship and enjoy him.

- As the writer to Hebrews reminds us, don't *give up meeting together, as some are in the habit of doing, but let us encourage one another…* Devote yourself to regularly getting together with God's people, both in regular worship and informal gatherings. We are not meant to depend on God independently! Rather, we will find that our rest is increased as we get together with others in our community and share the wonders of our great God. As we learn and grow together, we will be better able to rest in Christ.

- Set aside time to spend building relationships with people who are important to you. Make this a central part of your day off.

- As you grow in your relationships with others, figure out how to *encourage one another daily* (Hebrews 3:13). This might be through emails, phone calls, or online messages. Of course, we should not neglect encouraging the people who live in our house or that we see at work!

- Consider your work, and think about ways that God is using you through it in his work of provision and renewal. Cultivate a sense of God's purpose in your work, and look for further ways that he could use you in this arena.

- Consider the resources God has given you, and how God might be calling you to be generous with them—to help those in need and to further his kingdom.

- Think about a "Sabbatical" retreat you could take that would help you to experience God in a new way. This could be through a conference, or a service project, or a mission trip, visiting a spiritual retreat, or even making a pilgrimage. Or consider if God is calling you to give even more time: a year, a career, your retirement…

- Look back through your reflections through the study and see what other ideas you have come up with!

God is inviting you to enter his rest, to give up pointless work and exhausting relaxing, and to live a life filled with his purpose and presence.

Rest Definitions

1. Rest = contemplating & enjoying the Creator and his work
2. Rest = confidence that needs will be provided
3. Rest = knowing you are reconciled with God
4. Rest = assurance that God is renewing everything (even you)
5. Rest ≠ doing nothing
6. Rest = trusting in God's completed work
7. Rest = worship
8. Rest ≠ no difficult circumstances
9. Rest = knowing a loving God is in control
10. Rest ≠ doing whatever you want
11. Rest ≠ achieving spiritual perfection
12. Rest ≠ no effort
13. Rest = spending time dedicated to God
14. Rest = reflection and reconnection
15. Rest = a gift from God
16. Rest = encouragement given and received
17. Rest = regular realignment with God's will & works
18. Rest ≠ "Me Time"
19. Rest = finding pleasure in loving God
20. Rest = regularly stopping your normal work
21. Rest = sleeping sound in Jesus
22. Rest = meditating on God's works and Word
23. Rest = re-creation
24. Rest ≠ finishing all my work first
25. Rest = finding good works God has prepared for me
26. Rest ≠ laziness
27. Rest = work as the means, not the source, of provision
28. Rest ≠ having enough hoarded resources
29. Rest = trusting God's blessing by being generous
30. Rest = depending continually on Jesus

small group
discussion resources

Week 1 Session: Rest Self-Diagnosis

On the first week when you receive the books, take some time to do a "rest diagnosis"! This will help you to begin to get an idea of the areas of your lives God would like to address through this study.
Here is a suggested order:

- Tell people that you are going to look at case studies of some "rest-deprived" people, and that they should try to see which of them the most identify with. Have different people read the case studies aloud.
- **Ask:** Which person did you most identify with, and why? Discuss.
- Ask people to have pencils ready to mark on the list in Chapter 1. Have one person read aloud the beginning of the chapter, but when you reach the bullet-pointed list, read around the circle.
- **Ask:** Which of the items on the previous list are most true of you? Are there any other symptoms of "unrest" that you see in your life? Discuss.
- **Ask:** What would your definition of "rest" be?
- If you have time, read through the "Avram" case study at the beginning Chapter 2, as well as the next section entitled "Encouragement to Endure."
- **Ask:** Even though it is a much more extreme situation than most of us are facing, are there ways in which you can empathize with Avram, and the other recipients of the letter to the Hebrews?
- Read through Hebrews 4:1-11, found in the text of Chapter 2. Encourage people to read this each day over the next week (or even memorize it) to familiarize themselves with the text and concepts.   Over the next week, they should read Chapters 1-6 and answer the questions at the end of each.
- Encourage people to use the little prayer at the end of Chapter 1 daily, and pray it aloud together.

Week 2 Session: Resting in God's Completed Work

The principal idea of this week is that our rest is founded on God's great and completed works: creation, provision, redemption, and renewal. In each case there is a "work in time" that connects with an "on-going work": creation leads to provision, and redemption leads to renewal. It is in our perception of each of these as sure that rest rests. It might be good to begin with a review of this basic concept.

Here are some possible discussion questions for this week:
- What are some things in God's creation that you enjoy thinking about, looking at, or experiencing? How does this contribute your sense of rest?
- What might it look like for you to contemplate and enjoy God? How could this contribute to your sense of rest?
- What difference would if make if you really believed God was able to take care of all of your needs—apart from what you are able to do?
- What is some way that you have seen God provide for you unexpectedly in the past? What kind of anxieties are you currently experiencing about any needs that you have? (Your group may want to pray together for these.)

Note: *Provision* does not necessarily mean what we might call *Prosperity*. God wants us to depend on him for our "daily bread"—he does not promise us a luxury car. If people have questions about this, you might want to look at Philippians 4:4-19, and also re-read the last section of Chapter 4. We will also be talking more about our role in provision in the last week of the study.

- How does Jesus' finished work of redemption compare to the path to redemption in other religions? What is the mental or psychological effect of knowing this for certain? What impact does it have on your actions?
- Have you ever felt "performance pressure" to please God? What impact does this have on your relationship with God? What difference does it make to you to know that God accepts you as you are—even as he gives you the power to begin to change?

- How does knowing God is *"making everything new"* relate to our anxiety about global warming, pollution and other environmental concerns? What about war and suffering, famine and natural disaster? What other situations might this belief impact?
- For the next week, people should read chapters 7-12, and answer the application questions. They should continue to read the Hebrews passage daily as well! (Or even memorize it, if they wish...)

Week 3 Session: Resting By Faith from Self-Reliance

The primary idea in this week is that it does us no good to know that God's work is finished if we do not rest in it by faith, leading to worship of the God who is Rest. The opposite of this is self-reliance—what Hebrews calls "hardness of heart". This may manifest itself either in legalism, which results in anxiety and pressure to perform or license, which creates counterfeits of rest that fail to satisfy our souls.

Here are some suggestions for your discussion this week:
- You could, if you want, listen to Keith Green's old song *So You Wanna Go Back to Egypt* to review the Exodus stories of the water and the giving of manna.
- How did you feel about the people in these stories? What do you think they say about people's tendency to focus on their circumstances instead of God? What do they say about self-reliance and hardness of heart?
- **License** (like the Old Testament Israelites) is the way of thinking that wants to do what I want to do however and whenever I want to do it. It is relying on my own rest rather than entering God's rest. How is this evidence of disbelief and a "hard heart"?
- **Legalism** (like the New Testament Hebrews) is the belief that I can be righteous through my own actions, through obeying the rules, and through being better than others. It is relying on my own works, rather than God's completed works. How is this evidence of disbelief and a "hard heart"? Why are we attracted to legalism? What does it appear to satisfy in us?
- Pick one or more of the case study characters and answer the following questions about them (there are also specific questions in Chapter 7):
  - What evidences of self-reliance do you see in their life? What impact is it having on them?
  - What difference would it make to them to take time to contemplate God and his creation (of them as well)?
  - What difference would it make if they trusted God was providing for them?

- What difference would it make if they believed they could add nothing to Christ's work for them, and that God already sees them as perfect?
- What difference would it make if they believed God was renewing both themselves and the world around them?
- What beliefs do you have that may be blocking you from entering God's rest? How could worship change that?
- For the next week, people should read chapters 13-18, answering the questions and looking up the longer texts that are referenced but not quoted. They should also continue meditating on (and maybe memorizing) Hebrews 4!

Week 4 Session: Creating Containers for Rest

The primary idea for this week is that we need disciplines of rest—focused times devoted to Biblical rest—in order to help that rest permeate the other areas of our lives. This is primarily found in the concept of a once-a-week Sabbath, but we may extend these into daily disciplines, and into our leisure time too.

Here are some suggestions for discussion this week:
- What do you think about the idea of *containers* that was suggested this week? How are containers helpful? Which pitfall did you think you were most likely to fall into:
    o No containers? (No times set aside for Sabbath rest)
    o Confusing container and contents? (Focusing on the discipline itself rather than the rest itself)
    o Putting the wrong contents into the container? (Making my own selfish desires the primary focus of a day/time of rest)
    o Too compartmentalized? (Dividing time into "sacred" and "secular" rather than seeing it all as God's)
- What does a "Sabbath day" look like for you? What does it include or not include? Going to church/meeting with other believers? Not doing ordinary work? Spending time with family/friends? Spending time reflecting on God and his creation?
    o What obstacles do you face in observing a "Sabbath"?
    o What changes would you like to make in your life that would help you to have a real Sabbath rest?
- What daily practices do you observe to realign yourself with God and his work in the world? What practices appeal to you? (Refer to p. 86-87 for some suggestions.)
- What difference does it make to you to think of all your time as "God's time" rather than your own? How does this change how you see your leisure time? What would it take to make you come back from vacation grateful, instead of grumpy?
- For the next week, people should read the chapters 19-24, answering the questions and continuing to meditate on Hebrews 4.

Week 5 Session: Filling the Containers with Rest

The primary idea from this week is that we need to fill our times of rest—and especially times designated as Sabbath, dedicated to God—with the right contents if they are going to be truly restful, and keep from filling them with things that actually rob us of rest. We want to be lovers of God more than lovers of pleasure, and learn to rest from our work, alone and with others, enjoying his provision and presence.

Here are some suggestions for discussion this week:
- What do you think it looks like to be a *lover of pleasure rather than a lover of God* in your attitude toward leisure time? Are you afraid of God taking your pleasures away? What difference would it make to see the pleasures that you enjoy as God's gift? How does that increase your love for the Giver?
- What would it take for you to deliberately set aside your work for most or all of a day once a week? How would you have to prepare? What kind of mind-set would you have to have?
- Are you good at getting the physical rest that you need? What difference does it make to dealing with your troubles and temptations when you are physically rested or not?
- Do you have an easy or a difficult time meditating on God and his word? What stops you from spending time in worship? What practices might help you "be still" and focus on Jesus and what he has done for you? What difference do you think this would make to your ability to rest in him generally?
- Who are the people close to you that you would like to rest with? Who are some other people you might like to invite into rest with you, that you may not know so well? How could you lean into spending good social time with someone you are in conflict with?
- What kinds of activities do you feel "re-create" your soul? What are some you need to avoid, whether because you don't feel you can do them to God's glory, or because you too easily do them to excess?
- For the next week, people should read the last six chapters, and answer the application questions. They should continue to meditate on Hebrews 4 and drive it deeper into their souls.

Week 6 Session: Working Restfully

The primary idea for this week is that we work out of our faith in God's completed works—that is, we work out of rest. From there, we can search for the good works that God has *prepared for us to do*—works that are part and parcel of his completed work. We can also work meaningfully with him as participants in his great works of provision and renewal in this world.

Here are some suggestions for discussion in this week:
- Do you classify yourself as hard-working or lazy? (Of course, for many of us, we are sometimes one and sometimes the other!)
  - If hard-working, what drives you to work hard? In what ways do you run the risk of not resting as we have been looking at?
  - If lazy, in what ways does it show up? (Refer to the list on p. 115.) How is laziness actually the opposite of rest? What things does laziness produce that go against a rest in God's works?
- How does the idea that God has made good works just for you (and you for them) transform your idea of your work—at home, at school, on the job, volunteering...?
  - What do you think about the idea of a daily "treasure hunt" for the good works God has for you?
  - What are some "good works" that you think God has particularly made you for?
  - If you cannot miss the good works God has made for you, how does this change your attitude towards what you are **not** able to get done?
- How do you see God involving you in his work of provision— for yourself, your family, and others? Through the intrinsic nature of your work? How do you feel him challenging you in this area?
- How do you see God involving you in his work of renewal in the world? (See p. 112 for a list of ways we show renewal each day.) How has God called you to be an agent of reconciliation in your family and community? How could you prophetically show God's work of renewal to others?

Ask people to share one change they want to make in their lifestyle as a result of this study (you may refer to the suggestions in the Epilogue), and/or one change they have seen in their own heart as they have learned more about the "rest for their souls" offered them by Jesus.

Made in the USA
Middletown, DE
03 September 2017